Church

OF THE

Open Sky

ALSO BY NAT YOUNG

Surfing Fundamentals
Surfing Australia's East Coast
Surfing and Sailboard Guide to Australia
The Compete History of Surfing
Nat's Nat and That's That
Surf Rage

Church
OF THE
Open Sky

NAT YOUNG

MICHAEL JOSEPH
an imprint of
PENGUIN BOOKS

MICHAEL JOSEPH

UK | USA | Canada | Ireland | Australia
India | New Zealand | South Africa | China

Michael Joseph is part of the Penguin Random House group of companies
whose addresses can be found at global.penguinrandomhouse.com.

First published by Michael Joseph, an imprint of Penguin Random House Australia Pty Ltd, 2019

Front-cover photograph of Ryan Burch at G-Land, Indonesia, by Norys
Back-cover photograph of Bryce Young by Blair Jeffreys
Cover design © Penguin Random House Australia Pty Ltd
Text design by Louisa Maggio © Penguin Random House Australia Pty Ltd
Typeset in Sabon by Post Pre-press Group, Brisbane, Queensland
Colour separation by Splitting Image Colour Studio, Clayton, Victoria
Printed and bound in China by RR Donnelley.

 A catalogue record for this
book is available from the
NATIONAL
LIBRARY National Library of Australia
OF AUSTRALIA

ISBN 978 0 14379 671 8

penguin.com.au

To Tom Blake, the first surfer I knew
who had vision for what surfing really is.

CONTENTS

FOREWORD
WILLIAM FINNEGAN

Nat Young was famous where I grew up, on the beaches of Southern California. My family made the trek to San Diego to watch the 1966 World Surfing Championships, which Nat won, defeating my hero, David Nuuhiwa. Nat was only eighteen, a big rangy kid absolutely ripping on a mysteriously thin board he called Magic Sam. He wasn't a humble, aw-shucks type. He won a Chevy Camaro V8 convertible along with the title, sped off to Las Vegas to celebrate, wrecked the car, and didn't seem to miss a beat. A year or two later, he reportedly surfed First Point Malibu on a big south swell. I don't know how I missed it – those were my Malibu grom years – but everybody talked about it like a divine visitation. Nat had blessed our waters.

It must have been odd, being worshipped like that. I only realised how odd, though, when I picked up this book and learned that, while still a teenager, Nat started writing a weekly column for the Sydney *Sunday Telegraph*, and wrote it for the next nine years. A surfer barely out of school with a regular column in a major newspaper? That could not happen in the US, either then or now. Antipodal celebrity is different, I know – surfers count. Still, it's a bizarre measure of young Nat's extreme renown. Not only that, but Nat's mentor, Bob Evans, *also* had a column in the *Sunday Telegraph*.

Evans, a surf film maker and magazine publisher, comes off, by the way, in this account as a thoroughly charming fellow. He takes Nat on surf trips, introduces him to the Sydney business world, churns out films and magazines, and in Hawaii loved, of all places, dirty old overbuilt Waikiki. 'He would plan his whole day around the cocktail hour' at the Royal Hawaiian Hotel, Nat writes, where he would sip a mai tai and watch the sun set 'listening to Harry Lyman singing "Yellow Bird".'

Nat could have been a reporter. An eyewitness to several chapters of surfing history, he takes real pains to set down here his version of the shortboard revolution (though he abjures that term, for arcane reasons). In the standard history, there are only a few characters – George Greenough, Bob McTavish, and, quite centrally, Nat – driving the big transformation of our little world, but now he adds a dozen more, all furiously experimenting with variations on what Nat calls 'edge boards' in a collective breakthrough of design and performance that he neatly describes as 'diffuse'. Vinny Bryan, Bob Smith, Dana Nicely, the Value brothers – you won't find any of these names in the *Encyclopedia of Surfing* or, for that matter, in the collective surf memory, but here they get their due. And the main test wave for these experiments, we learn, was a single obscure reef on Kauai. Who knew?

Organised competition and surfing are an uneasy mix. Riding waves is, after all, much like dancing, the intensity of the experience can be quasi-religious, relatively few surfers compete, and the ocean is a wild, unlevel playing field. Nat has lived these contradictions more intensely than most. He started off winning a long string of titles, both in Australia and overseas, and then became, like Hamlet, a troubled philosopher prince, beset by ambivalence. He went country, living barefoot on the North Coast of New South Wales, still surfing his brains out and starring in surf films, but largely avoiding contests. Later, during the long-board revival of the 1980s, he re-emerged as a competitor – riding, ironically, the very type of board that he had once helped consign, we thought, to the dustbin of history – and completely dominated the new longboard circuit, winning four world titles between 1986 and 1990.

You can feel his double-mindedness throughout this memoir. On the one hand, we find him and the American *enfant terrible*, Miki Dora, agreeing that professional surfing 'would be the final blow for the art of surfing as we had known it'. And he is certainly right when he announces, on the first page of this book, that surfing is 'not a traditional sport . . . not something you do casually, like playing a round of golf with your mates on weekends.' (This point seems lost on the several billion people now trying to take up surfing casually, as it were, as adults. It doesn't work that way. It's all or nothing.) On the other hand, Nat argues at length for the idea that surfers should be paid for the commercial use of their likenesses – in films, in photographs. When footage of him surfing appears in a film (he can be seen in more than seventy-five films) and he is not compensated, he considers it 'in breach of my copyright as a professional surfer'.

The truth is, while he clearly worships sincerely at the Church of the Open Sky, Nat has also made a grand career. I notice him up in the National Portrait Gallery, with Gough Whitlam and Cate Blanchett. He spends the Northern winters skiing in Sun Valley, Idaho, where Ernest Hemingway ended his days. Like Hemingway, Nat came from nowhere in particular (Collaroy – he barely mentions his parents) and rode a huge wave of talent and determination into the spotlight, where he has spent his entire adult life. Not incidentally, he has managed to be in interesting places at interesting times, which has left him with a boatload of stories. So you should pull up a chair. The man they used to call the Animal has mellowed, somewhat, and he's had adventures in every corner of the world, with plenty of lessons learned, and he's ready to share.

PREFACE

I had no intention of writing another book, having written and published six books already.

Thank goodness all my books sold well – all, but *Surf Rage*. Not that low sales on that book really mattered to me. Compiling *Surf Rage* was good therapy while I was in recovery from an assault, an incident I dealt with in those pages. After I wrote *Surfing Fundamentals*, it made me feel good when people sent me thankyou notes from all over the world detailing how they'd learnt to surf from either the original version or the French translation. And *The Complete History of Surfing*, published in 1983, was a huge undertaking, as the history of surfboard riding had not been documented up till then.

No matter how I look at it, writing my books has always been a rewarding experience. But after completing my autobiography, *Nat's Nat and That's That*, released in 1998, I figured I was done. As with all my books (besides this one), it was self-published. *Nat's Nat* was written from diary notes, my mum's scrapbooks, and memory, and covered my life from 1963 to 1998. It reprinted four times before eventually falling out of print. Loads of people still buy it online as an ebook or an audio book. I had a plan once to read it in a recording studio to turn it into an audio book, but after reciting the first chapter I realised I was hopeless and really needed to work on it. I've since laid down all sixteen chapters of this book. I feel pretty good about the end result.

These last ten years or so, since I officially retired, I've been happy to sit back and enjoy my twilight years with family and friends, surfing and skiing. I enjoy writing the odd story for the *Surfer's Journal*; that Californian magazine consistently captures the essence of surfing. *White Horses* in Australia occupies the same category.

I still like the discipline of writing. I have great material in my diaries, and my memory is not too bad. I like telling these stories. It keeps my hand in, so to speak. Over the years a few punters have made contact, expressing how much they enjoyed *Nat's Nat* and wanting to know if I will be doing any more books. Perhaps it's my loose, unprofessional writing style or the funny stories – I'm not sure, but I have a sneaking suspicion it is a fascination with the '60s. Then again, it may be all the sex and pot that have made that book so popular!

For whatever reason, push came to shove a while ago and it felt timely for me to start writing this book. If I think back on it, the initial impetus was the magic number sixty-nine, and coming to terms with the fact that I was about to be seventy.

Our bodies are just like any machine: as we get older, the moving parts wear out and you either replace them or toss the machine. I'm not ready to check out quite yet.

1

SURFING IS NOT
A SPORT

I have never thought of surfing as a sport – not a traditional sport, anyway. It's not something you do casually, like playing a round of golf with your mates on weekends. It's much more of a drug, a lifestyle, a religion.

Twenty-five years ago, when our younger daughter Nava had just started school, she brought home her enrolment papers and we sat down to diligently answer the questions and sign them. It was all pretty basic stuff until we got to religion. For the past forty years or so, ever since my meeting with surfing pioneer Tom Blake, who I believe was the first to coin the phrase 'The Church of the Open Sky', I have never hesitated to tell anyone who asks that I am a member. So that's what we wrote in answer to the question on Nava's form from school that inquired about our religion.

During the next couple of days, when I quizzed her about the reaction from her teachers, she said there was no reaction. Years later, I asked a mate who was a teacher at that school and he said they all had a good laugh in the staffroom over our family's conviction.

And so it goes on. I have always enjoyed telling stories of our tribe. Even when I was young I would retell the stories told to me by my elders. It's a part of surfers' unique heritage that goes back to our bohemian roots, and I feel it should be preserved.

From my research, I've learnt that ancient Hawaiian royalty rode waves primarily for enjoyment. Surfing was called *he'e nalu*. The English translation for *he'e* is 'transforming from solid form to liquid form', and *nalu* refers to the motion of a wave. Hawaiians incorporated this return to liquid in a daily ritual for commoners and royalty alike. Both classes rode waves for pleasure, the commoners on their shorter *alaia* boards, and both classes held competitions. The royals rode their longer *olo* boards, and for them, the contest was to see which surfer could ride a wave from beyond the break into a floating marker near the shore. Whoever got closest won. It was good honest competition – not like today's contests with their subjective judging, where someone with dubious understanding assesses your performance. The common people had the same form of competition but, from what I understand, they did not mix with royalty.

Surfing was a day-to-day activity that most people engaged in at every opportunity. Everything revolved around riding waves, from the blessing of the trees that they used to make their boards, to the separate beaches they designated for royalty versus commoners. Surfing was even involved in courtship, as an intricate part of Hawaiian foreplay. It was the norm to ride naked on a wave with a girl you were interested in before making love on the beach.

Engraving of Wahine with *alaia* surfboard. ***Robert E. Van Dyke***

As hard as the Calvinist missionaries tried to stamp out surfing as a pagan act, it still flourished in many parts of Hawaii. After the overthrow of the Hawaiian kingdom in 1893 the popularity of surfing surged as more island people sought solace from America's political conquest.

Pre-contact, wave riding for pleasure seemed to be widespread throughout Polynesia. In his journal from the 1770s, the English explorer Captain James Cook described seeing men in a canoe riding waves at Matavai Point in Tahiti. After watching several waves being ridden to the shore, Cook concluded that the men were doing it for their personal enjoyment. The fact that they went out and rode more than one wave convinced him that they were not just returning from fishing.

In 1778, Lieutenant James King, an officer on Cook's ship, described watching twenty or thirty natives riding surfboards in Hawaii. On festive occasions, tribes would come together for gatherings called 'meets'. You would bring your woman, kids, food, dogs and your favourite surfboard to the beach to socialise and ride waves together. I believe the word 'surfmeet' originally meant just that: a meeting of like-minded people who enjoyed surfing and hanging out with other members of their tribe. When I first went to Hawaii in 1962, contests were called 'meets', and some older Hawaiians still say 'meet' when referring to surfing contests. In Australia, the first contests were called 'rallies'.

Before the mid-twentieth century, surfing was associated with Hawaii almost exclusively. Travel writers in the late 1800s and early 1900s, including Mark Twain and Jack London, wrote glowing reports of locals shooting the breakers at Waikiki. A wealthy American newspaperman, Alexander Hume Ford, became a big fan of Hawaii. After growing up on the east coast of America and travelling extensively all over the world, he moved to Oahu permanently in 1907. One year later, he founded the prestigious Outrigger Canoe Club. Situated in close proximity to Waikiki, it was a popular hangout. After a modest beginning as two grass shacks, it expanded, with a palatial clubhouse being built that featured a spacious outside dining room and facilities right on the beach. By 1914, the club, which was formed entirely for social reasons, had 1200 members and a long waiting list. Its membership came from the Honolulu elite and almost all of the members were white.

In 1905, a group of Hawaiians got together and called themselves the Hui Nalu – the 'Club of Waves'. Their membership consisted of local surfers, including the famous Hawaiian waterman and Olympic swimmer Duke Kahanamoku and his five brothers. Tom Blake, who originally came from the mainland, was one of the few white exceptions in the club. The outfit was very exclusive. Membership was predicated on skill in the water. Every potential associate had to be voted in by other members, and they had no clubhouse. Instead, they met under a big hau tree in the grounds of the Moana Hotel in Waikiki.

Hui Nalu, The Club of Waves. Waikiki, 1905. *Herb Wettencamp*

The Hui members were mostly known as 'beach boys' – locals who doubled as surfing instructors and lifeguards for the hotels. It's not surprising that there was some rivalry between the Outrigger and Hui clubs, even physical violence. Perhaps this was when modern competition came into existence. There certainly was intense water-sport competition between them, and surfboard-riding was an integral part of those contests. However, I have not been able to find out exactly what form the competitions took.

The Makaha International Surfing Championships started in 1954 with sponsorship from a local restaurant, and ran successfully until 1971. The event was shown every year on US national television from 1962 through 1965, introducing America to surfing competition. It was the unofficial world championship until the first official World Surfing Championship was held in Australia in 1964.

The first time the American mainland was exposed to surfing was in 1885. Three brothers, Hawaiian princes Jonah Kuhio Kalaniana'ole, David Kawananakoa and Edward Keliiahonui, were attending boarding school in San Mateo, near San Francisco. Riding 15-foot (4.6-metre), 100-pound (45-kilogram) boards, they paddled out at the San Lorenzo River mouth and put on a dazzling display in Santa Cruz. The local press covered their 'exhibition'. It seems hard to believe, but surfing remained dormant on the mainland for the next thirty years, until the Irish-Hawaiian surfer George Freeth gave another display of surf-riding in Huntington Beach in 1914.

Freeth had an Irish sea captain father and a native Hawaiian mother. He was born in Honolulu in 1883, and with his blue eyes and fair skin he stood out like a sore thumb. He taught himself to

The first international surfer, Hawaiian George Freeth, on the beach in California, 1907.
Photographer unknown

surf at Waikiki on a board he cut down from a 16-foot (4.9-metre) *olo* that his uncle gave him. With a bit of perseverance, Freeth became the most talented surfer in Waikiki.

To outsiders, surfing was new and exciting. The act of riding waves fascinated the general public but no one understood what it really was. Then the media stepped in and, trying to classify the activity, labelled surfing a 'sport'. There was nothing like surfing in Western culture. Skiing perhaps, but that was derived directly from European modes of transportation and any enjoyment, at first, was a by-product. The idea of viewing it as a pure form of pleasure was still in its infancy.

From what I can surmise, the media's 'sport' label was more or less adopted by society and has lasted until this day in the mainstream. But surfing could have gone in another direction very easily. I think surfing has all the ingredients to qualify as an art form or, as I mentioned earlier, a religion. In 1912, Tom Blake first met the great Duke Kahanamoku at a newsreel premiere at a movie theatre in his hometown of Milwaukee. Tom was impressed by the charismatic Duke and followed him to Los Angeles and on to Hawaii.

Over the next couple of years, Tom came to appreciate what the Hawaiians were doing when they went surfing. He became a close friend of the Duke and they hung out together, both on the mainland and in Hawaii. Tom even beat the Duke in a 220-yard (200-metre) freestyle swim. According to Tom, this made their bond even stronger.

Tom built his first board in Hawaii, an exact replica of the *olo* boards of the ancient Hawaiians. He had mixed success with that particular board but built many more for himself and his friends and even went into the surfboard-building business in California. Tom was good with his hands, working with tools such as an adze. He is credited with being the first man to surf Malibu. He also crafted the first water housing for a camera, which he bought from the Duke.

From a surfboard perspective, Tom Blake's greatest contribution was fin technology. He was the first person to put a fin

Tom Blake and Duke Kahanamoku, Waikiki, circa 1913. *Photographer unknown*

on a surfboard. Before this innovation, 'hard cutting', or angling across a wave's face, was problematic. 'Hot Curl' boards, with their deep vee in the tail, achieved this to some degree, but adding a fin enabled surfers to turn and angle across the wave-face every time – which is basically the foundation of all modern surfing. In 1928, Tom organised and competed in the first major American surfing contest at Corona del Mar. Like most surfers, he says that he went along with the 'sport' tag until he discovered the truth for himself.

When I met him in San Onofre, California in the winter of 1982, he explained how he had arrived at this time and place. At eighty years old, he was more than 6-feet (183-centimetres) tall and still strong, with striking blue eyes. He wanted to share with me what surfing represented to him. Tom had been a vegetarian for more than fifty years, stopping all meat in 1924. He said that surfers were the original 'back-to-nature hippies'. In his view, the purest surfers did not leave their footprint on the land. They did not pollute the environment, nor did they use up the earth's resources. In short, Tom believed that surfers were the chosen few. He lamented that as he got older, he could not handle the heat of California in the summer and spent the bulk of his time away from the ocean in Wisconsin.

He had published two books, *Hawaiian Surfboard* and *Hawaiian Surfriding: The Ancient and Royal Pastime*. After we had been chatting for a few hours, he handed me a copy of his amazing dissertation on the essence of what surfing meant to him. It was titled *Nature = God: The Voice of the Atom* and was a testament to his understanding of what surfing had become for him, transforming in his eyes from a sport to a religion. He told me his original, religion-themed essay, 'Voice of the Wave', was what *The Voice of the Atom* was based upon.

To summarise Tom's theory in a few words is difficult. He stated in his book that 'Einstein's cosmic energy field of matter is real, something that affects us. We cannot escape its reward or its sting. Much, but not all, depends on our own personal conduct and actions. Surely, sow and reap in kind has ageless truth. (It) is retroactive and so the net result of the 'Nature equals God' concept points up the absolute necessity of observing the rules of our species for survival and wellbeing.'

Just before he died in 1994 at the age of ninety-two, not long after I'd hung out with him in Southern California, I began to understand for myself what a spiritual pursuit surfing could be. A letter I received from Tom in March of 1994 helped shape my understanding of the essence of surfing. I think its message is still valid today.

In part, it reads: 'Nat, I note you mention embracing my pet philosophy theme Nature = God. Grateful for this, as the concept has far-reaching implications. It will gradually give the various religions over the world a better understanding of reality.' If anyone is interested, and happens to be passing through Wisconsin, there is a stone plaque that Tom carved prior to his death that reads 'Nature = God/Blake'.

Tom Blake's letter to me, Autumn 1994.

*

In the 1980s my wife, Ti, and I used to visit her Uncle Sid, aged in his nineties, every Friday afternoon. We used to take a couple of kilos of prawns and a bottle of beer to him. As we were leaving, he would always say to me, 'Hurry slowly'. It took a while for the meaning of that statement to sink in but I think I got it in the end. When you think about it, 'hurry slowly' could be applied to a turn on a wave or your whole life. It seems that everything is about speed these days: air travel, the internet, fast food, etc. People just don't take time to smell the roses. I sound like an old person, which I suppose I am.

I think body-contact sports are a form of entertainment from our past. They've had a good run, from Roman times up until now, but really they are passé. The football clubs treat their fans like brainless children and have no integrity, expecting blind loyalty. Think about that for a minute. One star player is traded to another club and the fans are expected to support the club regardless. Rugby, gridiron and all its derivatives are violent. How can mums and dads stand on the sidelines and watch their children potentially get maimed week after week? Why anyone would want to play a body-contact sport is beyond me.

My wife and I limited the amount of time our children played any of these sports, believing it was better for them to be with nature. We understood there were some benefits to playing team sports, but for us, the bad points outweighed the good. In a team sport, you have to rely on the other players. You are one cog in a wheel. That is a good lesson, but if you fail, you're letting the rest of the team down. Granted, coping with failure is an important lesson, and it makes winning that much sweeter. But I believe you can learn these lessons without violence. I suppose it comes down to how you want to learn them.

For our family, learning as an individual was the best method. As Tom Blake implied, it's important to understand that nature is God and you can be snuffed out in an instant by the force of a wave. Nature is not forgiving. Instead, it's honest and all-powerful. In that respect, you are nothing. That's the real story of what Blake was saying with his Nature = God philosophy.

Surfing slows things down, particularly in the tube. I know I am not alone in saying this. Nine out of ten surfers will say that to ride the tube is one of the ultimate experiences they search for on a wave. I think that more than 50 per cent of surfers in the world never get to ride in the tube – it's that difficult to do properly. Still, all surfers know what it looks like and they search for it almost every time they enter the water.

In the mid-1960s, when George Greenough figured out how to shoot motion footage way back inside the curl, everyone was turned on to what the tube looks like. His movies made the tube stand still. Time had no relevance. You could be in there for a minute, or ten minutes. In reality, most times it's just seconds. But you just don't know how long it goes on for. During a good session, time does not exist. That's what makes surfing so special. I have rarely met a surfer who says they get to surf as much as they want to: everyone wants more. You have no choice when you get into it – surfing becomes your obsession. All the surfers I know do it every chance they get. Maybe it's a drug. Once it gets you hooked, you have to have as much as you can get.

Dr Timothy Leary summed it up in the 1960s. 'The key to post-terrestrial living,' he said, 'is going to be grace and aesthetics . . . It's tied to surfing because it means that we'll be freed from gravity, and we can be totally into style and grace. And it may seem strange to be talking to surfers about post-terrestrial living, because surfing is water, and we're talking about air or a vacuum. But it's perfectly logical to me that surfing is the spiritual aesthetic style of the liberated self. The reason why I define myself as an evolutionary surfer is because surfers have taught me the way you relate to the basic energies, and develop your individual sense of freedom, self-definition, style, beauty, and control.'

In 2017, 34-year-old ex-pro surfer Bobby Martinez was asked about life after pro surfing in the *Surfer's Journal*. He stated that competition had led him to hate surfing. 'During my whole surfing career,' he said, 'there was no satisfaction the entire time. I hated it.' Bobby went on to say that 99 per cent of the kids who go through surf coaching programs aren't going to make it as pro surfers: 'It's like they are being intentionally set up for failure. I think it's pretty sad. I've seen kids come up the beach crying because their parents are pushing them too hard. That's not surfing. What are they doing that to their kids for?'

Back in March of 1982, my wife and I stayed a few days with Gerry Lopez in Hawaii while we were on our honeymoon. He was very gracious – a wonderful host. Every morning before we surfed he did yoga. 'I've been studying and practising yoga for a long time,' he explained, 'and I found that the state of samadhi [enlightened consciousness] can be attained through a regular and dedicated practice of deeply focused meditation. I've been a surfer for a long time too, and I believe that the focus necessary to surf successfully is also a state of deep meditation.'

When asked many years ago what surfing was to him, former world champion Mark Richards replied, 'Surfing can be anything you want it to be.' Mark has always been an excellent diplomat, never wanting to offend anyone, but this was a bit too noncommittal for my taste. I suppose you can call surfing anything you want. After all, it's only a label. In traditional sport, you have rules and boundaries. All the ball sports need a court, a field or a net to play the game. Surfing has never had that. Maybe it will one day, with the advent of wave pools, but real surfing will always be done on natural waves made by storms in the ocean.

Recently, I read a quote by the young surfer Dave Rastovich. He said, 'Anytime in my life when something challenging has happened, I've gone surfing and it's changed everything. That's why it's not just play. It's not just this silly thing we go do. It's more meaningful than that.'

In my opinion, a section I kept from a newspaper article in San Francisco, written by Jaimal Yogis, sums up the religious connotations pretty clearly. He wrote:

> So why does surfing appear to be so much more freighted with spiritual meaning than other water sports? One key distinction is the structure and pace of the activity. Yes, there are those brief adrenaline-pumping moments of actually riding a wave, but in between sets are long lulls when the surfer is just waiting, bobbing, staring at a horizon – time in which there's nothing to do but breathe and consider saltwater's flirtatious dance with the sunlight and sky. So, whether you're spiritual or not, there's still a need for a contemplative solitude in relative stillness. There's also the constant paradox of having to exert great effort to paddle, while simultaneously surrendering to the power of a wave you're riding (or falling into) – a Zen metaphor if ever there was one. All this may feed into why, when you look at the science of peak experiences, water and music are basically tied for first place.

William Finnegan's Pulitzer Prize–winning book *Barbarian Days* captures the notion of surfing as a way of life or quest, in part recounting the experience of Bill and his mate setting off from America to explore the world. Anyone who has a desire to understand the true nature of surfing should read *Barbarian Days*.

Recently, I stumbled on an interview with a man who is considerably younger than any of the other surfers quoted here. Garrett Parkes, the 27-year-old son of legendary New Zealand kneeboarder Dave Parkes, is from another generation. Garrett was always an incredibly talented surfer. Back when my younger son, Bryce, was having a crack at competition, he became mates with Garrett. Bryce would win a heat or Garrett would. They were both amazing to watch.

Bryce Young fully committed. *Al McKinnon*

Bryce stopped competing in 2010, but Garrett kept doing it with considerable success. He had good sponsorship from Quiksilver. However, one day a couple of years ago he walked out of the water after losing a heat and that was the end of that. 'I wasn't going to let competitive surfing ruin my whole vision of what surfing is,' he said. Garrett is a much happier man now. He surfs for pleasure. His parents have advised him to invest his sponsorship dollars wisely, and he's bought a rental property in Byron Bay. He is currently riding boards his dad makes for him and learning how to shape.

Think about this: no two hand-shaped surfboards are the same. For all the new designs made every year, every slight variation has been shaped by a dedicated surfer who is trying to enhance the experience on a certain wave. Californian Ryan Burch is one of Bryce's best mates. They are both in their mid-twenties, and whenever they get a chance they hang out, doing a fair bit of travelling all over the world. One particularly challenging adventure they went on was a camping trip: six weeks in the wilds of the Spanish coast with their good Basque friend Jokin. This wasn't some comfortable summer holiday. It was more of a battle with nature. In September and October, rain and sleet are a daily occurrence in that part of the world. Everything from the tent to their sleeping bags became a soggy sponge. The waves were big and strong in the Bay of Biscay, between Spain and France, requiring a lot of paddling against strong rips. These testing conditions suited both the boys. Their attitude is 'Surf anything – just make sure you have the right board under you.'

From my observations, Burch is a happy man provided he can surf and shape. He needs these two elements to exist. Ryan is addicted to making surfboards. He really can't help himself. On his four recent trips to Australia over as many years, he has managed to spend a couple of months each time at our house in Angourie. In between surfs, he spends his time building boards on our farm. During those years, he has probably built forty boards, everything from 4-foot 10-inch (1.5-metre) fish to 12-foot 2-inch (3.7-metre) gliders.

I have been on the receiving end of three of those boards. The first was a complete surprise. I was helping the boys unload a week's worth of Ryan's shaping production at Angourie one day, and I commented that the 7-foot (2.1-metre) asymmetrical I was holding felt a little corky for either of them. They looked at each other, turned to me and said in unison, 'Happy Father's Day.'

Ryan and Bryce had built that board for me. I had no idea I needed a new board, but they did. Sometimes I have been spoilt by the spirit of friends and family.

The surf was good at the Point that first day I laid the board down, and it felt right for me. I got a couple of corkers. I liked the feeling on the forehand with the one driving keel-style fin, and I liked how sharp it turned through the top with the quads under my back foot. I loved the horsepower and the handling. That board is stringerless, with carbon fibre on the rails to give it strength. Bryce probably has twenty boards with this same construction and I have yet to see one break, even under the pressure of a crashing, 10-foot (3-metre) lip.

The other board Bryce and Burch made for me was not such a surprise. We were all in California for my sixty-eighth birthday. It was November 2016 and the California Surf Museum was holding a celebration of the fifty-year anniversary of my first World Championship in San Diego. I knew the new board was coming. They were all excited and so was I.

The new shooter was another asymmetrical: 6-feet 10-inches (2 metres) with a wider tail and some volume. It looked like it could be a bit of a challenge for this old man. My son-in-law Taylor carefully packed it and carried it home to Oz. I tried to surf it in clean, 4-foot (1.2-metre) swell at the Point but failed to get a good wave. The problem wasn't the board – it was me. During the next session, I finally got a good one and immediately saw that the design was fantastic, though I feel 6-feet 10-inches is just a bit too short at my age. Probably all in my head, but there you go.

Ryan is unique in that he doesn't just shape a board and give it to a glasser. On special ones, he lays down the colour, glasses,

sands and wet-rubs – the whole nine yards. He also makes some
of the fins himself. While working on our farm, he was excited to
have offcuts of cedar and silky oak to shape his fins with.

Burch sees the future of his increasingly successful surfboard
business very differently from any other company I have known.
He intends to sell his boards for a higher price, keeping the profit
high and encouraging people to buy fewer boards and value what
they get. This business model seems to be working: at the time
of writing he is over a year behind in custom orders. Whenever
possible, he likes to be the first to try his creations, though I can
recall one occasion when we sat on the beach together watching
the way a new board moved under Bryce. It was a replica of a
Wayne Lynch design. Ryan made it a few years ago and it was
perfect: 8 feet (2.4 metres) long by 24 inches (61 centimetres) wide.
Other than Wayne's original, it's the only board I have seen that
looks like that, and it surfs like it's straight out of Paul Witzig's
classic movie *Evolution*.

It seems to me that there is a common thread with all these quotes
and the attitudes of the different surfers I have written about in
this chapter. Surfing should not be sold short by people in organi-
sations or the media, who, for the most part, are not surfers.
I believe there is an obligation to embrace our history, to tell the
real story of where we came from and to explain the ways surfing
can be appreciated as something wholly apart from a traditional
sport. Our heritage is unique and should come across clean and
strong, to give an honest impression of what surfing really is.

Bryce on his Burch-shaped Evolution board. *Jack Coleman*

Here are a few things to remember:

Every committed surfer should try to shape a board for themselves sometime. It is a unique part of our heritage that no other
sport has.

Contests are barely representative of the true surf experience.

Hurry slowly.

Make it a beautiful life – you only get one chance. (This is our
family motto.)

And finally, Nature = God.

2

THE REAL
MIKI DORA

I've already mentioned that I really like telling surf stories. I see
it as something I should be doing as a tribal elder. I've had the
chance to observe and surf with many different personalities over
the past sixty years, but none were as unique as the great Miki
Dora.

To me and thousands of other surfers, Miki was our James
Dean. I wrote about a few of our more bizarre escapades in my
book *Nat's Nat and That's That*. Some of the stories were so
amazing that many people thought they were bullshit – except
everyone who knew Miki knew they were true.

One thing's for sure, everyone who met Miklos Sandor Dora
III immediately saw he was a unique character, colourful beyond
words. He had an entirely different style from anyone most people

The great Miki Dora, with me, and Denny Aaberg, en route to have lunch with Miki's dad in Santa Barbara. I told that story in *Nat's Nat and That's That*. Denny's mum took the pics.

had ever met. All the facets that made up his personality were totally understandable, if you knew his background. He was cool, but he was a real scammer. Some people hated him, but others loved him.

I can say that he was a loyal friend, always making simple, credible sense whenever we talked out of earshot of anyone else. When other people were around, however, he spoke the 'Miki mumble'. It was a language all his own, invented to say nothing, but everything. It involved a lot of hand gestures and words I had never heard before. I saw his mumble in practice on numerous occasions in many parts of the world, and never tired of listening to him unload on a suspect. Mostly I just watched. It worked best with police officers and airline employees, or anyone in authority.

We did a bit of travelling together in the early '70s. Not all over the world, mind you, but to a few out-of-the-way places, including Nepal, Pakistan, and Afghanistan just before the Russians bombed the shit out of the Afghans. They wiped out a lot of the luminous greenery in the valleys and turned much of the countryside into a dustbowl. Miki and I loved hanging out with the local nomadic people.

The mountain tribes who live in that part of the world do not recognise established national borders. For example, if you look on a map these days, you'll see Tajikistan and Kyrgyzstan but not Pashtunistan. Pashtunistan is a country that has since vanished. We heard a great story about Prince Raci of Pashtunistan. He was invited to Kabul for a royal ceremony and managed to swoop on one of the wives in the Afghan king's harem. All hell broke out when he was caught and imprisoned in the jail in the capital. When word got out to his clansmen they stormed the prison, pulled down a portion of the old stone wall and took Raci home.

These people are warriors descended from warriors. They have been fighting wars forever. I do not believe anyone will ever conquer them – not the American government nor other neighbouring tribes. The West would be well advised to remember the Crusades in the Middle Ages. The people's attitude towards war is like dedicated surfers' attitude towards surfing: they do it every day. It is their life. Their only relief from war is the game of buzkashi, which is played on horseback with a headless goat.

When I visited these countries with Miki in the early '70s, it was my second time in a Muslim country. I had spent a few weeks in Morocco in 1968, but we had little contact with the locals. As an Aussie kid growing up on Sydney's Northern Beaches, I had no contact with Muslims. In my world they simply did not exist.

Miki and I extended our stay from a few weeks to a month. During that time, I came to understand how family-orientated Muslims are. Now, with numerous experiences over the past forty years, I have found that they are some of the nicest people in the world when you get to know them. It's understandable that some Muslims who live in the West feel marginalised. It's hard for us to put ourselves in their position. How would you feel if you were forced to leave your home country, or had to watch it be invaded over the centuries by outsiders? How would you feel if everyone seemed to hate you? Dealing with racism on a daily basis would be intolerable. Being glared at, called names, even spat on, you too may feel marginalised.

The thing that sticks in my mind from that adventure was the underground city between Pakistan and Afghanistan. With our trusty guide, we drove from Peshawar up through the Khyber Pass to Charsadda on the route to Kabul. At the border, we left the car and disappeared down an ancient staircase into another world. We did not get to see the whole town, but it was all built below ground, with shops, cafes and a huge market selling every type of exotic good, from performing bears on chains to giant hookahs to all manner of spices, fruits and vegetables. By following the crowd, we came back up the steps into Afghanistan.

I still have some mementos from that trip and they're as good as the day I bought them – handwoven prayer rugs, tightly laced with vibrant colours, and a roll of black-and-white woodblock prints of Tibetan religious stories, which Bryce and Ryan Burch have been glassing onto special boards.

Miki and I had contemplated travelling overland to Europe, but it was easier to go back to Karachi and fly to France. When we arrived in Paris, we split up. Miki went to Germany to pick up a kombi van and I caught the train to Biarritz. As I had partially financed our trip to the Middle East, I was starting to get low on funds and needed a place to stay.

Jean-Marie Lartigau was one of the finest surfers France ever produced, a seven-time French champion. He was only defeated in 1969, and that was when his younger brother, François, took the title. Jean-Marie completed his national service in New Caledonia and came to Australia in 1971, staying with my first wife and me in our old farmhouse in Byron Bay. He gave me the address of his mum in Biarritz.

After wandering aimlessly around, trying to make sense of the street signs, I was pointed to her house. Annie lived behind the Biarritz police station, within walking distance of the train and the beach. Since Jean-Marie was in Australia and François was travelling all over the surfing world, she seemed like my best option. When I knocked on the door of her apartment, she welcomed me with open arms and invited me to stay. I explained I was not flush with funds so a deal was struck: I would paint the inside of her house for room and board until Miki arrived.

Derick Disney and Bryce with special boards, featuring my Tibetan block prints. *Ti Deaton Young*

As it was autumn, the weather was getting colder and the storms were getting more consistent. I spent less time surfing and more time painting or getting a lift to the Barland surfboard factory in Bayonne. An Aussie mate named Richard Harvey was living in the Basque Country at the time. In addition to being a talented goofy-foot, he was also a very good surfboard shaper. We both built sleek guns of balsawood, cutting the board into three pieces lengthwise, then using a router to chamber the sections to cut down the weight. I called my board 'French Girl' and made the sticker myself. I took her to Hawaii, rode some really big surf and then took her to Australia, where I don't think I ever rode her. French Girl is on the wall at the Pacific Hotel in Yamba if anyone is interested.

Working on my balsa gun 'French Girl' in Barlands shop, in Bayonne. *Richard Harvey*

During that autumn, Annie Lartigau became a close friend. She would arrive home from the market just as I was getting back from my first surf and we would have breakfast and then I would start work, either painting or prepping, and she would sit and tell me of her life in Africa, of living in Niger, Senegal and Chad with her military husband. He was a doctor, a colonel in the special forces, involved in parachute jumping with the Red Berets. Both of her boys had been born in Africa. In addition to being gifted surfers, François and Jean-Marie were talented artists, using their abilities to support themselves. Up until François died of cancer in 2017, he worked for Quiksilver as a creative artist and was responsible for many of the designs in Quik's European clothing line. Jean-Marie, meanwhile, is enjoying his life on the Gold Coast with his family. After diligently paying his taxes in Australia until he turned sixty-five, he applied for and was granted a pension. This allows him to spend his days sketching and painting as much as his heart desires.

Eventually Miki came by after I had finished the painting, and I moved with him to the Hôtel du Fronton right on the square in Bidart. I was just learning how to hit a tennis ball, but Miki was nearly a professional. He was also incredible at golf and any other ball sport you can think of. After becoming frustrated with giving me lessons on a public tennis court in Guéthary, he dreamt up a scam to make the game more interesting for both of us. He thought about where we were and figured out how to exploit the situation.

His dream was for us to be able to play tennis at the exclusive Chantaco Tennis Club in St-Jean-de-Luz. Getting past the front desk was easy. Miki explained that we were visiting Americans, members of the Bel Air Racquet Club in Los Angeles. He was the resident pro with a desire to give his friend some instruction in the subtleties of the game. The guy at the desk was completely bamboozled by the infamous Miki mumble.

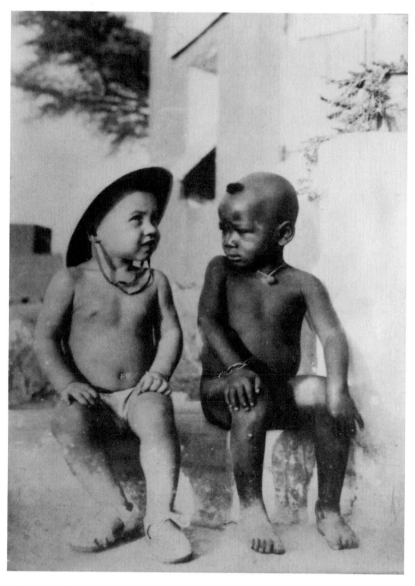

I have always loved this pic; it sat on Annie's mantlepiece in Biarritz. Jean-Marie Lartigau and his African friend. *Lartigau family*

We changed and went onto the court. Two mediocre players were hitting next to us. I was playing at my normal shitty level, and while retrieving a ball, Miki mentioned to one of the players nearby that he needed a real game, some serious competition; he was tired of giving lessons. He then suggested that we play the other guys. Just to make it interesting, it would be 100 francs a game. The French guys had seen how badly I played but had not witnessed Miki's skills, since he was deliberately playing down his game. They were nibbling the bait but had not swallowed it yet, so Miki flattered them by complimenting them on their form. Then he casually said that the standard of tennis overall was pretty poor in France compared to America. That of course did it. The national insult hooked them.

Now the story gets interesting. I am the fall guy, remember. I'm supposed to play badly, which is no problem. After the first couple of sets, we were down many more francs than we had. Miki pretended he was frustrated, venting that he really needed a good game, that it was just luck that they were winning. He challenged the best guy on the opposing team to a game of singles, this time for 1000 francs a game. They thought they had seen Miki play his best but he was still mis-hitting, playing poorly on purpose. He wiped the floor with the Frenchman. We ate out for weeks on that game.

On another trip to France, one summer in the '70s, Miki continually left highlighted newspaper clippings of the London stock-market report in my pocket. He was advising me to buy gold bullion and keep it in a vault in Switzerland. Even with the limited sponsorship funds I had at that time, I would have been a wealthy man if I had taken his advice. He did the same with silver, just as the stock price was increasing every day. Another lost opportunity on my part.

Richard Harvey with his beautiful balsa gun. *Richard Harvey collection*

In the late '60s, when I first moved to Byron Bay, I didn't have a
phone at my house so Miki used to call the local pub to reach me.
He would speak for ten minutes to whoever happened to be in the
public bar at the Great Northern Hotel, and then ask them if they
would mind driving up to my house, a couple of kilometres out of
town, to tell me that he needed to speak to me.

The first time he did this, I thought it was an emergency and
went tearing back down the hill. All Miki wanted to know was how
the waves had been in Byron. This was months before he told me
that his telephone would let him call anywhere in the world without
charge. Whatever system he had, it was absolutely free and he used
it for years.

Miki was a master forger. He had a perfect set-up for working
on documents in his apartment in Brentwood – a draftsman's
board with powerful lights. This was before credit cards and

computers took over the world. He could make perfect airline tickets back in the day when they were written by hand. He had a girlfriend who worked for Pan Am, and she procured the blank stock. I flew to Paris on one of Miki's tickets.

Miki in Kenya. *Miki Dora collection*

Once, in the mid-'70s, when Miki and another of his girl-friends, Linda, were staying on our farm on the North Coast of New South Wales, we had a bit of a problem. They were sleeping in my first wife's bedroom, with views looking up 80 kilometres of river valley. After Linda and Miki left, my wife went to get her passport and found it had vanished from her bedside table. I had my suspicions that Linda had taken it. She and my ex were similar in appearance: cute, short blondes with straight, shoulder-length hair. I choose to think that Miki did not know of the theft. I never brought it up with him.

Some people have surmised that Miki must have smuggled

drugs in the '70s to support his lifestyle. I happen to know this is not true. He told me he would never be so crude: dope was big and bulky and not worth the effort compared with gemstones. Miki carried diamonds from one country to another. He showed me some examples once, but since I had no education in this field, I could not appreciate the quality. He chose diamonds because they were small, valuable and easy to conceal. With all his international travelling, he developed an eye for quality. He knew where he could buy stones cheap in Africa and then sell them for a handsome profit in Europe or the States.

During his extensive travels, Miki came to love Jeffreys Bay in South Africa more than anywhere else in the world. Before his cancer had a debilitating effect, he spent much of his time riding the waves there and living on the point. When his King Charles spaniel died in a house fire at Jeffreys, Miki was devastated. He used to refer to Scooter Boy as his illegitimate son. Scooter was quite possibly the most well-travelled dog in the world. Before the indignities we are now forced to endure with airport security, Miki used to smuggle that dog on and off planes in a big black trench coat. Scooter Boy had been trained in Europe, where it is still commonplace for people to fly with their dogs – not many animals understood how to use airline toilets.

I never met Miki's stepfather, Gard Chapin, or any of his other surfing forefathers, such as Bob Simmons or the great George Freeth. I was too young to hang out with any of the old guard of surfing, aside from Tom Blake. The relatively younger crew of Californians from the '60s – Wally Froiseth, Jack O'Neill, John Severson, John Kelly and Dale Velzy – were not what I would call close friends. I only had limited contact with these legends. But from what Miki told me, all of these surfers first and foremost stuck to their core values, even though some of them, like O'Neill and Severson, were involved in the commercial end of surfing. Miki told me stories about growing up with Gard, watching Tom Blake living on the beach at San Onofre. According to him, they were all cut from the same cloth. Selfish, feisty individuals, they were outcasts from society – rebels, bohemian, independent, never with the same woman for any length of time.

The common thread was that they were all totally addicted to riding waves. Miki was not suggesting that every old surfer he knew was like this, just that the key players seemed to have a common thread to their lives. This is the real background of our surfing forefathers. They were not lilywhite yes-men. For the most part, they lived in their cars at the beach, catching food, experimenting with the design of the boards they made, exploring new breaks and having fun riding the waves they found. They were adventurers. Around every point there was another discovery. This same scenario played out all over the world, in every country where surfing took root. There are still some old surfers who are totally committed to the surfing lifestyle and are living the dream on remote outposts.

Miki Dora was all of the above, a product of his environment. It's just that his environment was the '50s and he adapted accordingly. When America discovered surfing for the second time in the early '60s, everything changed. An explosion of surf music and movies, and attention from the mainstream, turned his world upside down. He was forced to witness his beloved Malibu transform right in front of him. He could no longer live in his car at the beach all summer. There were loads of new surfers and tourists hanging around.

Surf Party promotion poster. Miki hated Hollywood and loved it at the same time. **Ryan Stopper**

He played along with the whole charade, of course. Just like Tom Blake, he did stunt work for the movies. Miki's dark good looks meant he could be paid pretty well for doubling for Frankie Avalon in *Beach Blanket Bingo* and other films. He hated the bullshit but loved it at the same time. 'I feel that hordes of kooks are creeping up on me,' he once told me, referring to Malibu at some point in the '70s. 'They're taking over my once-pristine point break.'

He resisted with all the stealth and cunning he could muster, but told me that surfing contests were the nail in the coffin. Once, during a contest at Malibu in the '6os, he took off on a wave from the point and pulled his pants down, then surfed right past the judges, bent over and gave everyone on the beach the moon. Miki believed that 'the essence of surfing had been turned over to a sea of imbeciles'. In his mind, it would never recover and would be lost forever if it was labelled a competitive sport.

As an example of Miki's fine mind, here is a quote from a story he wrote for the *Surfer's Journal*, titled 'The Aquatic Ape' and published in 2003. It took him years to write it and he worked with the aid of a thesaurus, just to keep everyone guessing about the meaning of some words. 'Fabricated surfing,' he contended, 'has degenerated into such a mockery of hypocrisy that it is almost impossible to recognise anything of merit. Now only the misled and misinformed determine social ostentation. The meridian that makes surfing stand alone from anything else on earth must be preserved, no matter how minute.'

While he did not believe in contests as they stood, he could see that with some changes competition could be made entertaining, unique and more representative of the true spirit of surfing. In 'The Aquatic Ape' Miki proposed a novel solution for surfing contests:

> This experience demands proficiency forthwith: the inventive skills and capabilities of the cerebrum and an individual's fortitude. Individual ingenuity is the solution to this enterprise. Non-sectarian, non-racial, non-sexist, open to the entire planet – if they dare try. When scrutinising the significance of this non-compromising event, the ramifications are

awe-inspiring. Firstly, this engagement will take place at Jeffreys Bay, South Africa, which is considered one of the fastest waves in the world. I will have total control over the menu and my decision will be final on all matters. I will make all decisions regarding time, place, wave size, conditions, et cetera. There will be no counter-productive judges (whatsoever). The purpose and aim will be to get from point A to B. In other words, the one individual, like a bat out of hell, who at top speed covers the longest distance, wins the esteem of the day.

All serious devotees who plan to launch into this engagement must place a Reliability Bond of $200 to prove competence [and] good faith, and to help verify that they're not biting off more than they can chew. This bond is refundable after the conclusion of the exercise, that's if the entrant engages throughout the whole test and actually rides more than 200 yards [183 metres]. All entry monies will be matched by myself and used for the aesthetic beautification of the area chosen by replanting indigenous vegetation including planting trees in probable ground-soil erosion areas.

Equipment: restrictions adherent to the apparatus used must be meticulously supported or disqualification will occur. All applicants must construct completely their own equipment from start to finish, taking written notations on the entire procedure. Also, video of the important steps in the production are required as a reference for authentication.

All equipment must be ozone friendly and biodegradable. Absolutely no petrochemical products may be used in any of the construction. No fluorocarbons or other harmful chemical processes. Nothing that might affect the physical condition and growth and development of natural organisms.

The ingenuity of the builder is paramount in this venture. Obviously, there are hundreds of possibilities and raw materials available, some thought of and some not. Just to bring to mind a scant few: balsa, the century plant family, veneers, natural glues, tree resins, pitch, tars, fibres, gum, rubber, fabrics, cloths, natural varnishes, wood dowels, chambering, rib construction, non-toxic gas injection, the hemp plant – it's endless. If surfers can be pried away from the one-eyed brain sucker, they can do it!

The only restriction on board design is that the maximum length cannot exceed 9 foot 6 inches [2.9 metres]. The tail must square off at 10 foot [3 metres].

Single fin only.

No logos on the board, whatsoever. No endorsements. No artificial devices to help keep the rider from slipping. Wax only. No colours. A clean stick is essential. Otherwise, anything goes, anything is possible.

Remember, this is a down-the-line speed test and going for distance. Design is essential . . .

Incidentally, only natural fibres can be worn – cotton or wool. No labels can be visible, no wetsuits, boots, gloves, et cetera.

And to keep everybody honest and upright, no leg ropes.

All subsidies, aid, support, patronage, endowments, donations, or sponsorships must be privately obtained with written proof.

If any government monies are involved in any way – whether local, state, or federal – automatic disqualification. Otherwise, I don't give a damn how you raise the money. Rob a bank for all I care.

No substance testing! Anything goes.

Like I stated before, no judges! There will only be a few official referee-estimators. Similar to a broad jump. Flagging the sand at the end of the ride. The furthest flag down-the-line wins the day. Clear cut, no disputes, one victor.

The entire progression will methodically take place on a minimum size of 8 foot [2.4 metres].

There will be no tents, food stalls, rock music, T-shirts, judging stands, bullhorns, fat hangers-on, groupies, pretenders, or any other commercial rip-offs.

Every entrant is entirely responsible for his own entity. The prize monies will be more than satisfactory to make up for any adversities. Self-reliance is the key to good fortune and conquest.

I don't know how surfers related to Miki's piece for the *Journal*. I choose to think that the readers found it entertaining. For me, it was more of a send-up of what pro surfing had become, with Miki giving his opinion as to how competition could be tweaked for the spectators and the participants. The idea was to take in the root of the activity and keep it, and separate it from the craziness of professional sport.

Competitive surfing today, predicated on judging and awarding points for manoeuvres, is ridiculous. Style should be the major ingredient. Miki's idea was to use speed as the yardstick. The fastest surfer from point A to B would win – a very honest way to find the best, if that is what you are trying to do, especially at a wave like J-Bay. The speed of that wave filters for talent. The best surfers find a way to ride it the furthest, and the fastest.

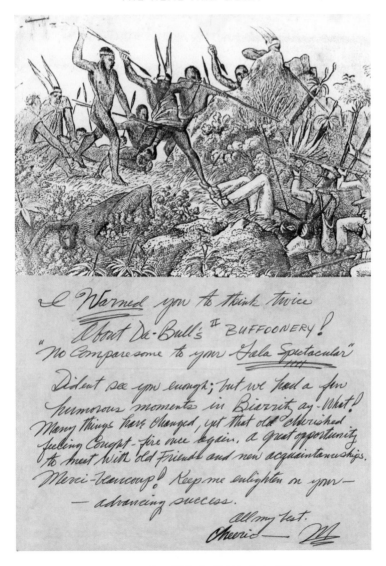

Aerogram to me from Miki in South Africa in April 1992.

Miki and I agreed that the rise of professional surfing would be the final blow for the art of surfing as we had known it all our lives. Never again would it be the rebellious activity that had captured the hearts and souls of a few thousand bohemian types in small pockets across the world. Now surfing would be mainstream.

I don't believe the millions of people who surf are really that interested in professional contest results. They may have enough of an interest to watch some of the television coverage, but it's not who wins or loses that captivates them. If they're like me, they just want to see good waves being ridden by competent surfers. Big-wave competition is another matter – everybody loves that. It is new ground, fantastic to watch, and only a select handful of surfers in the world are capable of pushing it to the next level.

Many people I talk to believe that surfers on the World Tour and the organisation that represents pro surfers are selling out our heritage, but you can't blame them. Those people see surfing as a sport, and it's how they are making their living. Undoubtedly the boys and girls on tour are talented surfers, but they are not the only surfers on that level. Everyone would agree they are among the top couple of hundred surfers on the planet, but there are lots of so-called free surfers who aren't on tour, who are also incredibly talented and often more aesthetically pleasing to watch.

3

COPYRIGHT

For as long as I can remember, there have been moans and groans from surfers about not being compensated when movie studios and commercial projects use their likeness. It goes back a long way – to the 1960s from my recollection, possibly much longer. Certainly the use of surfing for promotion and advertising exploded when the activity became fashionable with the Beach Boys, *Gidget* and Hollywood's discovery of surfing in the early '60s. Among my friends, loads of them top-line surfers, it's been a consistent topic of discussion.

How you feel about this issue probably depends on which side of the fence you sit. These days, pro surfers are paid very well to get exposure for their sponsors' products. However, other than the top twenty or so on the professional circuit, no surfer is paid directly for a picture of them. If you are outside of the top professionals, you are likely to be all for some compensation for your image being appropriated. On the other hand, if you are a photographer barely eking out a livelihood for the time and effort you spend taking pictures, you probably endorse the law as it stands. A photographer has the right to take both movie and still pictures of someone surfing and owns the resultant images. No compensation has to be paid to the surfer. This may change, but right now it is the law.

The Endless Summer, the late Bruce Brown's iconic surf documentary, followed two American surfers, Mike Hynson and Robert August, as they travelled the world in search of the perfect wave. Filmed in 1961 and 1962 and released in 1964 in America, and worldwide in 1966, it is still the classic surf movie and has grossed over $40 million. Brown put in a tremendous amount of work to make it. He mortgaged his house to pay for production costs and, when it was finally complete, went on the road in America for over a year narrating live at every showing.

The original deal was that the surfers would buy their own air tickets around the world and Brown would pay all their other expenses. Hynson was a few years older than August, more hip, and had allegedly been smoking a bit of dope for years. August was more the Ivy League student. Of course it was inevitable that Hynson would have a falling-out with the more traditional August and Brown.

After the financial success of *The Endless Summer*, Hynson and his then wife, Melinda, contacted a lawyer in Los Angeles. Together with August, they took their grievances to Brown, who (in addition to being the director) was the producer and owner of the movie. Hynson was stoked that everyone liked the movie but failed to understand why Brown had not even paid him back the $1400 airfare that Hynson had paid out of his own pocket; apparently August's dad, Blackie August, had paid for Robert's ticket.

The late Bruce Brown, who filmed, produced and narrated *The Endless Summer*. First released in 1964, it grossed over $40 million. **Brown family**

The meeting between Melinda, Mike, Robert and Bruce took place at Bruce's home in Dana Point. Bruce could understand their grievances and offered to set each of them up in a business of their choice and give them $5000 apiece and a new car – in my opinion, not a bad offer for the late '60s.

August took the deal and opened a surf shop. The offer was, however, unacceptable to Mike. His lawyer stayed in contact with Brown's, but required funds before he would pursue the case any further. Meanwhile, Mike and Melinda were getting more and more frustrated. They did not have any money to commit to the case, so they packed everything up and took off to Hawaii for five months. When the case finally went to court in Los Angeles in 1995, it was immediately kicked out on the statute of limitations: too much time had passed. Hynson continues to grumble to this day, while August feels fine about the whole *Endless Summer* experience. He views it as having been a win-win situation for everyone involved.

My own experiences with Bruce Brown and *The Endless Summer* were much more pleasant than Hynson's. In 1962, I was just turning fifteen and Paul Witzig invited me to go on the Australian leg of *The Endless Summer* shoot, a surf surfari to Western Australia. Of course it was a big deal for me, being a typical Aussie kid from a working-class family who had done nothing more than show a bit of talent for riding waves.

The other young surfer invited on this adventure was my school chum Rodney 'Gopher' Sumpter. Gopher and I were really good mates. We hung out together and stayed at each other's house on weekends. We were the same age and in the same class at Narrabeen Boys High School. When the day finally came to leave, we laughed as we drove away from Sydney. We figured that even if we didn't get any perfect waves, the trip would be a great way to get out of school for six weeks and go surfing with your best mate.

Paul had met Bruce Brown in Hawaii in 1959 while Paul was surfing and Bruce was filming that classic sequence of Phil Edwards in *Surfing Hollow Days* on the west side of Oahu. Paul and Bruce must have hit it off pretty well, since Paul was given the green light to shoot the Australian sequence for *The Endless Summer*. Armed with an old Bolex, a tripod and reels of film, we set out due west from Sydney in Paul's Volkswagen kombi van. Alongside all the stuff mentioned above, plus a pile of personal goods, we had a huge projector on board. It weighed a tonne, was old and solid, and took up half the kombi. The plan was to barnstorm Bruce's last movie to pay for the trip.

After two long days of nonstop driving we arrived in Port Augusta, smack dab in the middle of South Australia. Up until that point, I don't think any of us realised how far it was across Australia, or how far we still had to go to get to the west coast. In Port Augusta, Paul decided to put us all on the Trans-Australian Railway, including the kombi in freight. It was a hell of a contrast to bumping up and down in the cramped van, and Gopher and I loved every minute, sitting back in comfort for two days watching the desert slip by all the way to Perth. Paul was in his white-linen-suit and gin-and-tonic phase. We played up to that, pretending we were his spoilt little brothers, to the amusement of the other passengers.

After the movie showings in Perth, the true adventure began. We headed south to the Margaret River area and drove down every dirt track we encountered. We spent two days camping in complete isolation on a beautiful wide bay with perfect little lefts off a rocky reef. To this day, I have never seen the footage of that part of our sojourn. It was the best part of the trip to WA – but maybe it was just a figment of my imagination.

Eventually, we were all getting pretty gritty so Paul checked us into the luxurious Caves House in Yallingup. The next day, Gopher and I tried to paddle out at the infamous big-wave spot of Margaret River. The surf was probably only 8 feet (2.4 metres), but I remember there was whitewater everywhere. As a couple of Sydney grommets, we were way out of our league. We pushed on further south and did find a few smaller waves more to our liking at Ocean Beach in Denmark. It was pretty flat that day but I do recall there was a sign on the top of a cliff that read 'Killer Waves / Beware'.

We drove to Kalgoorlie, put the car back on the train, and after another two days ended up back in Port Augusta. From there, we drove to Bells Beach in Victoria, which is where Paul filmed the only wave of me that made the final cut of *The Endless Summer*. The shot shows me falling off the front of my board and the narration is a typical Bruce Brown send-up: 'Young Aussie Nat Young has to go one better than the Americans' hang ten. He is seen here hanging body.' At first I thought it was a complete embarrassment, but I loved Bruce's style and laughed when I saw it in the completed movie. Driving across Australia for one shot seemed like an awful long way to go. I guess that's the movie business.

Another classic Bruce Brown one-liner I can remember from the film came when he included a shot of a dachshund. The dog was walking along the beach at Pipeline, his penis dangling in the sand. 'We called this dog Sandy Dick,' Bruce commented. Everyone loved *The Endless Summer*.

*

Late one evening in 1993, Bruce called and asked if I wanted to help out with his new movie, *The Endless Summer II*. He explained that he was hesitant to do it as he was completely happy with life on his ranch, surfing, riding motorbikes and collecting Hudson motor cars. The only reason he'd agreed to take on the project was to give his son Dana a head start in the movie business. Bruce was calling me from Hollywood, sitting in a room with an executive of one of the biggest movie companies in the world. New Line Cinema was financing the production, but Bruce would have the final say on the cuts in the finished product.

Mike Hynson **Brown family**

It was agreed: New Line would pay me $10 000 for playing the part of being me. On top of that, Bruce said he wanted me to come up with ideas for what the movie's stars, Wingnut Weaver and Pat O'Connell, would do when they stepped off the plane in Brisbane. Nissan or Toyota supplied two brand-new four-wheel-drive wagons. Bruce said he wanted my son Beau involved in the shoot – for that, Beau would get a few grand – and we would play everything by ear, just like in his original movie. For Bruce, it was a proven formula.

He was a classic character. I always liked him and had tremendous appreciation for his dry sense of humour. We had lots of laughs shooting *The Endless Summer II* – from running away from aggressive crocodiles with Steve Irwin, to sliding the odd snake into Wingnut's sleeping bag.

I have a couple of stories that most people have never heard from *The Endless Summer II* shoot. The first one is from the sequence in Africa. You'll recall that several lions are pursuing a dune buggy in a game park. The boot of the dune buggy contained the carcass of a dead sheep, which was what was attracting the lions. A few months later, the son of the owner of the lion park was out feeding the animals when they turned on him, mauling him badly. The old man who had started the park was a fearsome character, tough as nails, who had earned loads of money hunting big game all over Africa. While on safari somewhere in Kenya, he was just getting back to sleep one night when a few lions started roaring close by. He grabbed a lump of wood and left the camp to sort out the fight. He had been there before and thought he had a special connection with that particular pride. According to other people in the camp that night, there wasn't much of a commotion. The lions turned on him and ate his body in its entirety.

The next story is from Costa Rica. It involves a beautiful amphibious vintage aeroplane called a Grumman Goose. New Line Cinema had contracted to hire the plane and its pilot/owner for one week. The insurance was to start on a certain day but the pilot flew down a few days early. The day before the shoot was scheduled to start dawned clear and bright. Everyone was on set so they thought why not go for it and shoot the sequence? The pilot was an ex-military test jock and a bit cocky. He wanted to show everyone what his amazing plane could do, and took it upon himself to try and land in the estuary at Tamarindo.

The area was way too small for any error. As the movie shows, one pontoon strikes the water first and the other closely behind, throwing the plane off balance. The pilot applied full power, trying to take off, but he should have killed the engine. The Goose struck the beach at full speed and was virtually destroyed. An old surfer friend of mine, Mike Diffenderfer, had gone along for the joy ride and ended up breaking a finger when the plane hit the beach. He was fortunate nothing more serious happened.

Since the shoot was not supposed to start until the next day, the insurance was not current. It looked like a nasty court case was in the making, but the producer of the movie agreed to pay $50 000 out of his own pocket. The hull of the Goose sat there on the beach at Tamarindo for two years until it was finally salvaged and taken back to the States. The funny thing is that there was only one shot planned to include the plane, and that was for Wingnut and Pat to stand on the beach, looking at the surf, while the Goose roared overhead just above the palm trees. The script didn't say anything about landing in the estuary.

*

Anyway, back to the discussion of whether a surfer should be able to lay claim to the use of his likeness.

In a packed courtroom in Los Angeles in 1999, the sportswear company Abercrombie & Fitch won the day with a decision that found it was completely within its rights to publish a picture it had purchased from the estate of the late LeRoy Grannis. However, this initial win was turned over on appeal. In the new ruling, the surfers in the shot were granted compensation for their likenesses being used in an A&F catalogue. The surfers, it seemed, objected to the manner in which the photo was used, without their consent. They stated that the picture, which had been taken in 1962 at the Makaha International Championships, had been presented alongside images of naked and scantily clad women and caused them embarrassment and shame. As sporting celebrities, they argued, their image was tarnished. They received substantial compensation.

In the US, the next landmark incident involving surfers and their likenesses was not taken to court. It concerned Laird Hamilton's amazing 'Millennium Wave' at Teahupo'o, a ride that redefined the parameters of big-wave surfing. After some fiery exchanges between the photographer, Tim McKenna, and Hamilton's manager, Jane Kachmer, it was agreed out of court that the parties would jointly share the copyright for the image, and all revenue would be split fifty-fifty.

In 2013, my attention was drawn to the esteemed New York publishing house Rizzoli and the iconic Australian surf photographer John Witzig, brother of filmmaker Paul Witzig. Rizzoli is in the business of publishing high-quality art books and they wanted to do a book on surfing. The only stipulation the publisher insisted on was that every surfer whose image was used in the book would need to sign a release. Its lawyers were hesitant to include photos without a release, since copyright law was changing in the States.

Most surfers signed the release, including me. John has always been supportive of everything I have attempted. He is also pretty good about donating prints of his photos to charity. But he gets understandably miffed when companies use his photos without contacting him. Recently a French company began selling a pillow using one of John's shots without his permission. They could have asked first. Now they'll have to deal with his lawyer.

While on the subject of pillows, there are two beautifully embroidered cushions available in Australia and America: one of Gerry Lopez and the other of me, showing various aspects of our lifestyle. Gerry's wife, Toni, and my wife, Ti, have both purchased these pillows. We are flattered with the end result but no one ever asked for permission. Perhaps it's not unlawful, but it strikes me as a little cheeky. It would have been nice to be asked.

Robert August (left) and Mike Hynson, in a publicity shot for *The Endless Summer*. **Brown family**

My interest regarding surfers' rights has been consistent over the years. Many of you will be familiar with the opening lyrics from the song 'Open Up Your Heart' in the movie *Morning of the Earth* that claim that there's no guaranteed formula for happiness. I remember the premiere at the old Manly Odeon in '73. It was monumental. From the first bars of the song, everyone in the packed theatre knew the film was a winner – the first honest exposé of where surfing was headed.

Owned and produced by Alby Falzon and David Elfick, the movie had three elements that created its ambience. First and foremost was the music. David had been the Sydney editor of *Go-Set* magazine and had close ties with the music world in Sydney and Melbourne. He coordinated the music, bringing some of the talent to his studio in Palm Beach, New South Wales on a few occasions to help them understand surf culture. The main man calling the shots on the score was G. Wayne Thomas. The other musicians wrote their songs, drawing inspiration from the footage of us surfing.

The next essential element was Alby's unique style of photography. He was very arty, very intrusive, as you can see from my sequence in the movie – tight close-ups of my life on the farm in Byron and slow-motion, blurred images of me surfing at Broken Head and Lennox Head. He learnt his art during his time in the army and under the tutelage of Bob Evans, the original surf-movie maker in Australia.

Of course, the third element was the surfers. We were an essential part of the movie's success – some would suggest the major ingredient.

After the film's initial success, Elfick sold his 50 per cent equity to Alby and went on to produce blockbuster movies such as

Newsfront. By that time, I understand *Morning of the Earth* had grossed in excess of a million dollars. Thomas, who had been contracted to produce the music, was paid handsomely. Some of the musicians, however, are still grizzling forty years later. In contrast to the surfers, they were at least paid something for their time, effort and talent. The surfers in *Morning of the Earth* received absolutely nothing, although I think Rusty Miller and Steve Cooney did receive a free trip to Bali. I still feel strongly that the surfers deserved some remuneration for their contributions.

When I brought this up with Alby some ten years ago, he laughed – not in a nasty way, though he was genuinely amused that I thought we should be paid for our time on screen. Alby has always been a self-styled back-to-nature guru. He lives comfortably, at least in part, on his investment of the profits of *Morning of the Earth*. As the status of the film grew with surfing's popularity, it became the yardstick for surf movies in Australia. *Morning of the Earth* was a revelation for the millions who had turned their backs on traditional sport, validating their pursuit of this selfish indulgence – surfing. The movie gave credence to the depth of our culture and what a surfer could achieve by simply living the dream of riding waves with total conviction.

Over the years, I have had a few discussions with Alby on the topic of compensation. One was when my friend Baddy Treloar was having a particularly rough time. Baddy was the surfer who sanded the board on the farm and ran down the track at Angourie to try it out. I asked Alby to pony up a couple of grand for Baddy, but he did nothing about it.

A few years ago, Andrew Kidman brought out a new movie that many of you may have seen called *Spirit of Akasha*. The publicity for the movie claimed it was 'celebrating *Morning of the Earth*'.

Its opening shots featured footage from *Morning of the Earth* of me surfing a Whale Beach wedge, followed by other footage from Broken Head. Neither Kidman nor Alby contacted me to ask my permission for use of the footage. I was not even sent a copy of the movie. I consider this to be rude and in breach of my copyright as a professional surfer. In every one of my books, I have had a budget for photographs and all the photographers were paid handsomely. For example, for my autobiography Alby was paid more than $2000 for his photographs of me. His only comment was to say that this was very generous.

When I sought legal advice on this topic, my friends in the Lawyers Surfing Association said that too much time had passed since *Morning of the Earth* and I stood little chance of getting a good result.

A few years ago, I received a cheque for a couple of thousand dollars and a thankyou letter from Greg MacGillivray, who made the most successful American surf film of the '70s, *Five Summer Stories,* and went on to produce and direct a stable of wonderful documentaries with Imax. When I shared this information with Alby a year or so later, he laughed once again.

Back in the late '60s, I recall that Wayne Lynch was upset with Paul Witzig because Wayne had had to sell his land in Victoria to pay his travel expenses – a trip around the world – for the *Evolution* shoot. Mark Richards had a problem with Dan Merkel over the use of a classic image of Mark on the North Shore in the '80s.

Some filmmakers think that the exposure of a surfer in their films enhances that surfer's deal with his or her sponsors. This is true in this day and age, when professional surfers are paid hundreds of thousands, or even millions, of dollars in sponsorship.

The Right of Publicity law in the US prevents the unauthorised commercial use of an individual's name, likeness or other recognisable aspects of their persona. It gives an individual the exclusive right to license the use of their identity for commercial promotion. The key to the law is *commercial* use. It seems that surfers don't have a right to their name or likeness when it appears in the *Surfer's Journal*, for example, or some documentaries that are not for profit, because those are not 'commercial' uses. An example of this is the Miki Dora case – he sued in *Dora v. Frontline Video, Inc.* in 1993 for appropriation of his name and likeness. *Frontline* is basically a news show and they made a film that covered events of Malibu in the early days. Miki lost that case not because he didn't have a right to his name and likeness, but because the use was not deemed commercial.

For the surfers before this new era, it was tough to support your lifestyle. In America, the copyright law has changed in the past fifteen years – but only for images employed for commercial use, not for the subjects of photos in editorial pieces. The laws in the States now recognise that it takes the talent on the wave *and* the photographer to produce the end result, therefore they jointly own the copyright to the photograph. The simple fact of the matter is that to make a great movie or image, it takes high-performance surfers working with a talented cameraperson and all the other necessary elements to create something of value. It is my belief that they should share in any rewards.

Surfers do have a right to their name and likeness in most commercial scenarios, but when it comes to enforcing those rights they are handcuffed.

4

MIDGET FARRELLY

If you ask any older Aussies about surf stars in their youth, the majority of them will only remember one name: Midget Farrelly. Midget was the first Australian surfing champion, and a true champion in so many respects. The only son of English migrants, he always said he was really thankful that his family settled in Australia after spending short periods of time in Canada and New Zealand.

In Sydney, the family moved into a suburb named Frenchs Forest. I only went to Midget's family home once. It was a modest brick-and-fibro residence that looked exactly the same as all the other houses on the street. It was approximately twenty minutes from the closest beach, and about the same distance from the Sydney CBD. It was well situated for Midget's dad, who drove taxis for a living. In order to go surfing, Midget had to take two different buses – over half an hour of travelling – to get to either Manly or Freshwater. His mum was a dance instructor and his sister, Jane, followed in her mother's footsteps, becoming an accomplished dancer. Jane was also a beautiful surfer in her own right and married the famed Australian big-wave surfer Bob Pike.

17-year-old Midget Farrelly with his best mate Kevin Platt at Freshwater. *Kevin Platt family*

How Midget got into surfing was a very natural progression. When the family first arrived in Sydney, his uncle, Ray Hookam, took Midget surfing at Bondi on his 18-foot (5.5-metre) paddleboard. Right from that first wave, Midget was addicted. He spent every possible minute riding waves at Manly or Freshwater, on his own and with his best mate, Kevin Platt.

At 5 feet 8 inches (173-centimetres) and beautifully proportioned, Midget had the fine-boned body of an artist. The way he held his hands and tilted his head always made me think he looked like he was dancing when he walked the board and executed his classic drop-knee cutback. Every facet of his fluid surfing was unique. He was always absolutely controlled and stylish. Put quite simply, Midget was the benchmark for good surfing in Australia in the early '60s. I don't believe that anyone who saw him ride a clean, open face on one of his sleek, 9-foot 6-inch (2.9-metre) longboards would have failed to be impressed. As one of the young, impressionable grommets at Collaroy Beach, I thought he was the best surfer in the world, and so did all of my mates.

In 1962, Midget won the Makaha International Championships. There was no official title at that stage but in Australia he was hailed as the unofficial world champ. However, he was not regarded as such in Hawaii or America. That particular year, the contest at Makaha was held in small surf, and in Hawaii, success in big waves makes you a champion. Still, when Midget came home to Australia, the media went ballistic. He was touted as the world champion on TV, in the newspapers and on radio, and became a household name in Australia, synonymous with surfing.

My relationship with Midget is a subject I have wanted to write about for ages. It's been churning inside me ever since his untimely death in August 2016. I feel fortunate that I got to the top of the competitive surfing pile in Australia just after Midget's own ascension.

I was considered the top dog on the competitive surfing ladder for years. In 1966–67, I won every contest I entered, including the Bells and New South Wales titles, the Australian Championships and the World Championship. The highest place Midget achieved in 1966–67 was second in the Mattara Surf Classic in Newcastle, and third in the 1967 Australian titles. He surfed well in the 1968 world titles in Puerto Rico and finished a close second to Hawaiian Fred Hemmings. That same year, in the Australian titles he finished third, I came in second and Keith Paull won. Midget also finished runner-up in the 1970 world titles in Victoria; I came in fourth.

By this stage, I was living in Byron. I had good sponsorship in the States and was over the whole competitive scene. I wasn't even sure I would compete in the New South Wales titles when I left my home and drove south for the competition. But the waves were so good for the contest at Narrabeen that I pulled on a singlet and won pretty easily. A similar thing happened at Bells that year.

I reckon Midget and I were well past our use-by dates in 1971, and neither of us competed. We were put out to pasture by the likes of Keith Paull, Peter Drouyn and Michael Peterson. I felt fine about giving someone else a go – all the better if he was a mate. Really, it is such a short time that anyone can be the best at any activity. My thinking was ride it, enjoy it, but know that there is always going to be someone better biting at your heels.

The last time I was close to Midget was in the Northern Hemisphere winter of 1963, on my first trip to Hawaii. He assured my parents that he would keep an eye on me, just like a big brother. He was three years older and it was my first time overseas. Everything was new and exciting. Before this, Midget had taken me on a couple of road trips to contests in Australia – Bells Beach and Newcastle. We drove in his brand-new 179 Holden station wagon. He was such a beautiful surfer, and on those trips he became my hero, both in the water and on the beach. With his Pommy background, he knew all the characters of *The Goon Show*, a radio comedy produced by the BBC. I had listened to the Goons on the radio every now and then, enough to play any part convincingly. As a method of whiling away the hours on the road, we dropped into the roles of Eccles and Bluebottle, which certainly helped make the kilometres fly by.

I'd won my initial trip to Hawaii by finishing first in the 1963 Australian Invitational Championships. Midget didn't compete in that contest because he already had a sponsored ticket to Hawaii. The Australian contest was held at Bondi, with huge crowds of spectators and media. As a junior competing in the seniors, I felt I was extremely lucky to win. However, it was a pretty hollow victory: everyone in the surfing world knew that Midget was the best surfer in Australia at the time, the true Australian champion.

That trip to the Oahu North Shore was my first experience in really big waves, and I was terrified. We rented a house on Ke Nui Road, right in front of Pipeline. It was just the three of us – Midget, me and another fine Sydney surfer, Kevin Platt. On many nights, the house shook with the pounding surf. It was Midget's second trip and he knew the ropes and made all the decisions about where and when we surfed. He took us out of our comfort zones and pushed our limits, which made Kevin and me much better surfers. I recall one heavy discussion about the importance of conquering your fear. Kevin and I took Midget's advice to heart.

Midget first, me second and Bob McTavish third. Happier times. *Young family*

Then one day it happened: a nightmare session when we were caught outside at Sunset Beach just before dark. The surf was so big we were already hundreds of metres beyond the normal line-up. We continued to paddle over giant wave after giant wave, desperate to get as far out to sea as we possibly could. Then the whole horizon went black and we saw that the bay was going to close out. The noise was deafening – a towering mass of white-water about to engulf us. At the last minute, all three of us stood up on our boards and dove off, swimming as deep as we could before the turbulence caught us underwater. Remember, there were no leg-ropes back then.

When we finally popped up we were all shell-shocked. I was exhausted and glad to have Kevin and Midget within sight. Every surfer who has been in this situation knows what I am talking about. I can still remember that swim: the roar of an incoming wave, me constantly turning and looking for either Midget or

Kevin in the fading light, then diving under another mass of white-water, being rolled violently underwater and coming up gasping for air. Survival was everything. You just had to keep going, keep swimming towards the shore, listen, look, dive under, come to the surface, and do it all again. It felt like it took an hour of swimming, fighting the rips, to get to the beach. We stuck together as the darkness descended, retrieving our boards a good 500-metres away from where we had paddled out.

Bob Pike (left), Midget's brother-in-law, and Dave Jackman, with their new elephant guns, about to paddle from Dee Why to surf German Bank off Long Reef, 1962. **Bob Weeks**

Most of the time, during the North Shore winter of 1962–63, the swells were big and from the north. We spent a lot of time driving to Makaha on the west side of Oahu. The local people had always eaten sea turtles, and many nights after surfing Midget, Platty and I were invited into their houses to share this treat. The only problem was that I had never eaten such rich, sweet meat.

On about the third night, I was reluctant to take my normal huge helping. All eyes were on me as I explained that I hadn't gone to the toilet in three days. A big Hawaiian at the table commented that I had 'one stuck shit, brah'. Of course everyone was laughing.

In the mid-'70s, a powerful lobby group of conservationists managed to get the eating of turtles totally banned in Hawaii. Understandably, the locals were pissed off – but the tiger shark population was delighted. With the abundance of turtles on the menu, the numbers of tigers exploded. More and more shark attacks occurred all over the islands. With sharks mistaking surfers for turtles, Mother Nature was out of balance. Strange that many of these attacks are not reported. They are bad for tourism, I suppose.

I do not know what I did to offend Midget personally, and I can't say what eventually ignited the so-called feud between us. Firstly, I defy anyone to find a bad word written or spoken by me about Midget – not in my previous books, not in any movie, not in any interview. I understood the situation was bad for Australian surfing and was poison for both of us. He said I was 'a brazen, conniving, ruthless, megalomaniac'.

The only thing I ever said to a newspaper was when a reporter asked me about Midget's complaints regarding the scoring of some silly contest. I believe I replied that Midget was a 'whingeing Pom'. I was just being silly and, in retrospect, unthinking. 'Whingeing Pom' was a nickname given to English people back in the '60s when they complained about conditions in Australia. Perhaps he took offence. He had told me that his parents were ten-pound Poms, having migrated under assisted passage. But honestly, who gives a rat's arse?

Here is an interesting tale that I have told at many dinner parties but never put in print. One winter's day in 1984, I was returning from a morning editing session in Sydney on my movie *The History of Australian Surfing*. At the time, I had not spoken to Midget since that trip to Hawaii in 1963. The deal was that the Australian Film Commission would reimburse me for travel expenses relating to production. I was flying in the local seaplane up to the city from Palm Beach (where I was living at the time) and returning when it suited me.

On this particular day, I left Watsons Bay earlier than normal in order to catch a possible quality wave at the northern end of Palmy. The wind was still offshore and the swell quite strong. I had spied a good sandbank towards Barrenjoey on the flight up to Sydney earlier that morning. On the return, my wife Ti came around the bend past the golf course, right on cue, to pick me up as the old Beaver taxied to the wharf. We drove up over the bluff to check the surf. No one was surfing. The waves looked pretty good and there was only one vehicle in the car park. I recognised it as being Midget's orange kombi. I asked Ti to pull over next to him and stepped out of our car. Midget was sitting in the driver's seat and I motioned him to wind down the window. He rolled it down halfway and, after some small talk, I said I would like to have dinner and talk about our problems. I explained I was genuinely sorry for anything I had ever done to offend or embarrass him.

I put out my hand to shake his and he did not take it. He looked me in the eye and said, 'I really like being your enemy.' That's all he said and I will never forget it as long as I live. I couldn't think of anything to say, so I just shook my head and slipped back into our car and we drove away.

Ti had heard what Midget said. Until this point, she'd had no idea about the intensity of his hatred. A lot of people didn't. Certainly he was very vocal about what he thought of me, expounding to anyone who would listen. Ti and I talked about it and our conclusion was that it was his problem – it was his cross to bear and I shouldn't go anywhere near it. It was a bitter poison that he would carry with him for the rest of his life. I know that I was not the only one to incite these feelings in Midget, but I believe I bore the brunt of his attacks.

Ti and I were in the snow country in Australia when a friend on the peninsula called to tell us of Midget's death. I decided I would not go to his paddle out at Palm Beach. Maybe I should have, but after all the bad blood between us, I would have felt like a hypocrite. Some mutual friends believed it would have been a good thing for Australian surfing. I understood their feelings, but the reality was that during the past fifty years, our relationship had been non-existent.

More than most people, I knew and understood what a fine waterman he was. I heard that in his later years he enjoyed his grandchildren, taking them on surf trips and teaching them about the ocean. I felt pleased for him, since the joy of being a grandpa is a wonderful thing to experience.

Back in 1967, when I first moved to Palm Beach, Midget was already living on the peninsula. My wife and I lived there for many years and so did Midget and his family. In fact, my wife grew up in a beautiful house right on Palm Beach. Since they were around the same age and both learning to surf, my daughter Naomi became best friends with one of Midget's children, Johanna. One day Naomi took my wife's new bicycle for a ride up to Midget's house to visit her friend. She put the bike down in the driveway at their house and Midget's wife, Bev, accidentally backed over it. You would have thought that would deserve some explanation or even an apology, but it was never mentioned. It was a strange way to handle an incident like that, for the kids as well as the parents. Midget was a strange, complicated man.

With the narrow two-lane road between Newport and Palm Beach, it was inevitable that our paths would cross coming from or going to Brookvale, where we both worked every day. Every time I saw him coming towards me, I would take a hand off the wheel and acknowledge him. Not once did he ever extend this courtesy to me. After a few months, I just gave up.

Midget Farrelly Surfboards sold as many boards as he could produce as a one-man band, doing everything meticulously in his small, two-room shop just five minutes from his Palm Beach home. His shaping was faultless. The craftsmanship is still some of the best I have seen. Everything was kept spotless in the workshop: not a tool was out of place.

As the business grew he needed more space, so he moved to Brookvale. Seeing a hole in the market, he went into the blowing of foam blanks. Surfblanks was jointly owned by Midget and a surfer/accountant from Bondi, Warren Cornish. After a short time, the company went to the wall and the partnership crumbled, later re-emerging with Midget owning the business outright.

One possible key to his hatred of me could be that I was outspoken in my support for the smoking of marijuana. I was, and still am, an advocate for legalising pot and have said so publicly on many occasions. In the early '70s, *Tracks* magazine was the platform for what the youth were getting into. Certainly, soft drugs were a theme of a few stories. Midget saw the attitude of the editors, John Witzig and Alby Falzon, as being totally irresponsible. I wrote a few articles on the topic and he must have felt they were irresponsible as well. I can say that anyone who was openly condoning the use of drugs felt Midget's wrath with a vengeance.

When Midget was pushed by a journalist on what I had done to him, the only thing he could ever say was that in Hawaii, on that first trip, I did not pay my share of petrol money. Honestly, I have no idea if that is true or not. Even if it was, I was fifteen for God's sake. His reaction seemed like a poor excuse for flat-out jealousy. In retrospect I believe it was on that first trip to Hawaii that the rot set in. When we left Australia Midget was my absolute hero, but when I saw the American legend Phil Edwards surfing the North Shore I couldn't help but be impressed, and I had a new idol to look up to. That's just what kids do, but apparently it did not sit well with Midget.

If Midget was jealous of my success, it would have been a crazy notion. Him being jealous of me would have been as ridiculous as me being jealous of Michael Peterson when Peterson took over my position as the best competitive surfer in Australia. As I said earlier, no one can be on top forever. Surely there was room enough for both of us to share the limelight.

I believe that competition is the fuel for jealousy. Losing is something that everyone has to deal with, and some do it better than others. The act of winning is easy to accept, especially if everyone is singing your praises. Midget was an intelligent man. He must have understood how being the top dog was fleeting. I still have trouble even rationalising his jealousy, but I understand it's a terrible problem for a lot of people. It just seemed to totally consume him. Two words would set him off and those words were 'Nat Young'. I know many journalists were flabbergasted by his venom. Many times I was asked what I had done to Midget; they thought it must have been something diabolical.

We were both inducted into the Australian Surfing Hall of Fame in the same year, 1986. He refused to go and accept his award because I was invited. The next event we were both invited to attend was the fiftieth anniversary of Surfing Australia, in Darling Harbour in 2015. Midget called the CEO, Andrew Stark, at the last minute and told him that if I came he would not show up. Andrew explained that it was his loss and Midget never spoke to him again.

You wouldn't have thought things could get much worse between us, but they did. The fifty-year celebration of his victory at the first World Surfing Championship was held in 2014 in Manly. The official committee, who had put months into the planning of this event, contacted me, offering to fly Ti and me down to Sydney for the dinner and the presentation. The committee, and many people outside the surfing world, thought everything was cool between Midget and me. They had no idea.

When Midget got wind that I was coming down for the celebration, he told the committee that if I came he would not show up. What were they to do? He was the guest of honour. The head official called me and explained their dilemma, and I told them I understood. I'd always hoped that, over time, Midget would let it go, but the celebration was really a party to honour his success, and if he felt that strongly about me being there, I would stay home. After all, I had seen it all before. Naturally, I was not happy with this outcome. I feel like all these incidents compounded and damaged the public image of surfing. Unfortunately, this was the way it was throughout my entire adult life with Midget.

In 2018, Ti and I accepted an invitation to go to the Sport Australia Hall of Fame annual dinner in Melbourne. Given Midget's passing, it was the first time in twenty years I felt like it would be cool to show up. In the past, I knew questions would have been asked about our relationship. He was the first surfer to be inducted into the Hall, in 1985; I was inducted in 1987. It's an honour for surfers to be included in this legacy of great Australian athletes. We have an impressive list: as well as me and Midget, there's Mark Richards (1985), Tom Carroll (1992), Pam Burridge (1995), Wayne Bartholomew (1999), Barton Lynch (2000), Layne Beachley (2011) and Wendy Botha (2018).

Midget never went to any of the awards dinners. I went to the first one and then stayed away. I felt embarrassed about the whole thing with him, and that surfing could be portrayed to the public in such a demeaning fashion. All that is water under the bridge now.

It felt good to write this chapter. It had to be done, but I do not intend to discuss it with anyone ever again.

The perfect 'Head Dip'. Midget Farrelly giving a demonstration at Bells, 1963. *Col Blunt*

5

BOBBY BROWN, PLATTY, EVO AND A TRAIN GOING WEST

Bobby Brown lived on the south side of Sydney Harbour at Cronulla, and I was from Collaroy, on the north side. He was a good friend of mine, although we didn't spend a lot of time together. In the old days, you had to drive for more than two hours, right through the heart of Sydney, to get from Collaroy to Cronulla.

The first time I actually hung out with Bobby was in the parking lot of the Dee Why Hotel one Saturday afternoon in the early '60s. All our mob had been surfing in the morning at Long Reef. When the wind came up, we grabbed a pie and took off for the closest pub for the afternoon piss-up. The guys who owned the cars made all the decisions about what we were doing. They were the alpha males, and as young blokes we just went along for the ride.

I don't know whose car Bobby was riding shotgun in that weekend. I seem to remember a hot goofy-foot named Garry Birdsall being involved. He was the only one I recognised walking in through the beer-garden gates. I was with a guy named Bomber Mills. He was a drifter, a master of keeping his head down and blending in. He lived in a big black duffel coat and his board shorts most of the time. When it got colder, he put on a baggy one-piece jumpsuit he'd bought from the disposals store in Dee Why. They were called 'bear suits' and all our crew at Collaroy had them. They were ex-flying suits, second-hand but still with years of good warmth in them.

Bobby Brown on the nose at his home beach, Cronulla. *Bob Weeks*

I think Bomber lived in his car. He never said where he came from. He didn't come from any beach in particular. One morning he turned up at Collaroy driving a big, soft, tan 1938 Dodge. Classic car. Perfect for going on surfari or just cruising the Northern Beaches.

Because Bobby and I were far too young to go inside the pub, Bomber said he would get us drinks and bring them back to the car. We were stoked and eagerly handed over our coin. We were gonna get pissed, just like the old blokes.

Bomber came back with a bottle of stuff called Barossa Pearl. It was sweet and bubbly, and tasted like medicine. We kept passing the bottle between us, taking bigger swigs. It went straight to our heads. I learnt later that drinking wine like that, out of a bottle in the back seat of a car, was something you only did with a girl when you had an endgame planned.

We had just finished the first bottle when, right on cue, Bomber opened the car door and handed us another one. Bobby and I were both gone, laughing hysterically. We were totally pissed but had managed to not throw up all over the back seat of Bomber's sled. I can't recall how I got home, but somehow we both stumbled back into our normal lives in Cronulla and Collaroy.

I did not see Bobby for quite a few months – contact with some people when you didn't own a car was limited. The next occasion I got to spend time with him was on a ten-day trip to the North Coast of New South Wales and southern Queensland that same winter, when Bob Evans was shooting his movie *The Young Wave Hunters*. Evo invited Bobby, Kevin Platt, and me to go on the trip with him. When we pulled up, Bobby was waiting on the side of the pavement where the Mona Vale Road joined the Pacific Highway, sitting on his little bag with his trusty board by his side.

Our Collaroy crew at Long Reef, 1962. *Barry Stark*

Bomber Mills with his sled. *Young family*

When Evo had told me that Bobby was coming with us I was completely stoked. I hadn't seen him in months. We got on well together and it turned out to be one of the best trips up the coast I ever had. The old Pacific Highway was a two-lane donkey track in those days. We had to cross two major rivers on punts that carried cars and their passengers – one at the Hastings River, south of Coffs Harbour, and the other at the Clarence River, near Yamba.

Just before boarding the second punt we turned hard right, driving down the southern side of the mighty Clarence, exiting just before Yamba. There were 3 kilometres of dirt to Angourie, then the road dissipated into sand dunes just past the dump. We pushed Evo's new Holden station wagon through the dunes and continued on to what is now the Blue Pool car park.

Scrambling over the rocks past the old quarry, headed in the general direction of breaking waves, we were totally awestruck by the perfect little lines pouring into the Point. We surfed it for two days, playing chasings on the beach and pulling the sand in around our chests to get warm before paddling back out again.

Kevin Platt was always a cool customer. Not very tall, only 5 feet 5 inches (165 centimetres), he always had a durry (hand-rolled cigarette) hanging out of his mouth and kept his cards close to his chest. He had the same style in the water – didn't crouch or bend his head any more than necessary, just stood straight and stiff. He could execute a perfect stall. Whitewater crashing all around him never washed him off, and he didn't have a hair out of place in or out of the water. Platty's style was smooth and precise, just like that of his dad, Lance, who had been a champion ballroom dancer with Platty's mum, Jean.

December 1962

A passing traveller might say, "What a lovely scene," but the first boardman to see Angourie could only say "KING, KING, KING!" Location: Angourie, near Yamba; eight feet south swell; light south breeze.

Discovery in The North

Twenty-five years from now when a surfer powers across the wall at one of the new thriving resort communities on the North Coast, probably his last thought will be for the person who opened up this new area to surfers.

You might say is it really important—Surfing World knows it is, and we aim to put it on record now that we have pioneers in our midst.

Easter of this year, saw the greatest exodus of surf board men ever to leave Sydney in search of the surf. Frustrated by crowded beaches, overcrowded waters, no parking places, and other controls, the enthusiastic "surfie" (like his compatriot "sports friends" the fisherman, the spearmen, boatmen, water-skiers and other refugees from

pressure) are seeking newer and more secluded pastures, and finding with relief, that they exist in great numbers on the magnificent beaches of the north and south coast of N.S.W.

Your Editor was typical of these explorers, and this story describes how we travelled and where, what we found, and who made the scene.

Just after the big wet of April we loaded our Falcon with food, cameras, boards, fishing gear and children and wheeled out on to the Pacific Highway.

After fighting the nerve racking bends and narrow roads to Gosford, we by-passed Newcastle, slipped through Raymond Terrace, gratefully increased our speed and headed for Buladelah, regarded by those

in the know as the staging camp to pleasure. The sub tropical jungles of the Buladelah mountains squeeze the highway and a tremendous rain forest of giant trees give us a welcome relief from the tall buildings of Sydney, and remind us of how young this country's development really is.

Just through Buladelah, we turn right to Bungwahl and soon leave the asphalt behind, more low mountains and suddenly the wide expanses of the Myall and then the Smith Lakes, with the Hamlet of Bungwahl indicating our turn-off to Seal Rocks.

It's a rough seven miles into Seal Rocks, but the seclusion and beauty of this place make the trip worthwhile. Here we met up with many

Surfing World Dec '62, Angourie. **Young family**

For me, Bobby was the star of those sessions at Angourie. He fitted right into those little tubes. Crouching low with his arms outstretched, he tore along the inside section. We didn't see another soul. It was a real adventure, going up and down the east coast of Oz in the early '60s. In the '50s there were five punts between Sydney and Coolangatta and also two tick gates, which were abolished in the mid-'70s.

Bob said he used to come to the North Coast with his brother Dick and their dad. Dick was actually the first outsider to ride Angourie. The local fishermen had long recognised the deep hole behind the rocks as one of the best spots for hooking up huge snapper. Some more adventurous members of the Yamba Surf Club had paddled their toothpicks down there to ride a few waves on their knees – really only training for the club surfboard races. In the local pub one afternoon, a fisherman turned Dick on to their secret spot. That next day, he caught a 5-kilogram fish and cooked it on the deserted beach for his family's lunch. After the picnic, he bodysurfed the perfect little curls running around the Point for hours, all on his own. Naturally Dick told Bob, and Evo wrote a story for his magazine, *Surfing World*. We were lucky to see Angourie at its pristine best – it would never be that way again.

We crossed the New South Wales–Queensland border and stood peering out at the lines of swell pouring into Greenmount, completely amazed – we had never seen anything like it before. Bob proceeded to shoot some film of us hanging out at Greenmount Point, and then we headed straight for Currumbin Alley. He thought the waves would be better up there and they were – crystal-clear water and wafer-thin little curls.

We surfed for hours and then checked into the Paddle Wheel Motel. It was one of Evo's homes away from home. I remember he always had a separate room, the same one every time. He knew the couple who owned the place. Over the next few years, we'd stay there many times.

Altogether, I made a total of seventeen trips up the coast with Evo. Just as soon as he could see a break in his work schedule we would be off, either that same day or the next. I never really knew when we'd be going. Sometimes we got away late in the day and other times early in the morning. He would call my parents' house and I was always ready to go – up at the crack of Dawn. (Unless you are an older Aussie you won't understand this reference. Bobby Limb was a celebrated game-show host in Australia and his assistant (and wife) was Dawn Lake. It's a pretty obscure connection!) Every year it was the same program. The first week of May I had to be ready to leave, whenever word came through that Evo was ready.

Not long after our first trip up the coast, Bobby defeated Midget Farrelly to win the 1964 New South Wales Championships. A few months later, he made the final of the first World Championship at Manly. Beating the great Midget Farrelly didn't go to his head, however. He stayed the same – a talented surfer and a very humble man. He was working as an apprentice carpenter and had a beautiful brunette fiancée named Lorraine.

Then, on 19 August 1967 when he was twenty-two years old, Bobby Brown was killed in an argument over a pool table at a pub close to his hometown. I was gutted. Everyone in the surfing world was. How could something like that happen to a soft, gentle guy like Bobby? Clarence Robert Tasker, who was thirty-one at the time, admitted to lunging at Bobby with a half-full beer glass, but that was all he admitted to. Tasker must have come to his senses soon after running the glass into Bobby's throat – he was actually the one who took Bobby to Cronulla's Sutherland Hospital.

Tasker was acquitted of murder in the District Court: his defence successfully argued that it was an accident. Apparently the witnesses were too drunk at the time to shed any more light on the circumstances. Either that or they had an obscured vision of what happened. Tasker did have two priors, convictions without jail time. One was for hitting a policeman over the head with a milk bottle. Neither count could be mentioned in Bobby's case since they were seen as being prejudicial. Prior to 2006 the Crown did not have the right of appeal in a criminal trial for murder. It must have been extremely distressing for the Brown family, not to mention Bobby's fiancée.

Kevin Platt also died in tragic circumstances, in 2000, basically from cirrhosis of the liver. He had been dead for nearly a week before he was found on 24 August. In his report, the coroner stated that Kevin was a chronic alcoholic. When his family went to his home in Casino to pack up his belongings, it was clear to them he had been living destitute. By this stage his mother, Jean, was in a nursing home in Casino and his father, Lance, had died.

I knew Platty pretty well back in the '60s, but only as much as he wanted me to. He was three years older than me and, like I said, pretty secretive. Kevin and Midget had sort of chaperoned me on my first trip to Hawaii. When they were kids, Midget and Kevin had been close. They were the same age and started surfing together at Freshwater. When I first knew them they also worked together, shaping for Keyo Surfboards.

Kevin had a neat FJ Holden and a couple of times took me surfing with him. I was riding a board with a hooked tail that Midget had shaped, an asymmetric that was advanced for the day. I remember a pretty session at Long Reef's second bombie. There were only a handful of guys out, with a stiff north-easter fanning a 5-foot (1.5-metre) south swell. Platty was ripping – smooth, stylish, perfect trim, and clean stalls in the curl, just like on the trip to Angourie.

Through his shaping, Kevin ended up being good mates with Bob McTavish. They were travelling up and down the coast every few weeks, shaping boards wherever there was work. They moved from house to house in the Noosa Heads area in the late '60s. Kevin's mother was quite domineering, a piece of work – she wore the pants. She sewed up the original board shorts in Australia for all of us. Later on, when Kevin got into heavy drugs, she was in total denial. There was no way her boy would be doing anything like that.

Kevin Platt, Jean and Lance. *Platt family*

By 1968, Platty had moved to Noosa and managed to persuade one of the most beautiful local girls to go out with him. Sue Davis was eighteen, a real stunner and a fine surfer. One weekend, Jean and Lance invited Sue and Kevin to come to Sydney to get to know her better. Within a few months the two were married.

Right afterwards, in 1969, they moved into what I always thought was the most beautiful house in Noosa. The Tudor house was a classic Davis home looking out over the national park. The Davis and Walker families were both old Noosa money, and close friends. A good portion of the prime property from Main Beach to the national park was owned by either the Walker or the Davis family.

Lance and Jean left Sydney and moved up to Noosa to get away from the rat race and stay close to their only child. Who knows how it happened, but at some point, Platty turned to heroin. I had lost touch with him by then. I certainly didn't know that he was using. Sue says she didn't have a clue either. She was working nine to five for Walkers Real Estate and getting up just as Kevin would be coming home from a party.

When they eventually talked about his habit, Sue told Kevin she could not see any evidence as he did not have any needle marks on his arms. He took off his watchband and showed her where he'd been injecting himself. Their marriage failed in 1977 and Kevin got involved with another beauty, Vicki, who had a daughter, Sian. He went on to father five kids with Vicki: Devina Rachel, Micah, Daniel, Joel and Promise. He had the big family he'd always wanted. Platty was drinking pretty heavily at this point, however, and it was impossible to maintain any sense of normality for the family. Vicki left him more times than you could count, but she always took him back.

Somehow Platty kept shaping. Kevin Platt Surfboards had a retail shop on Hastings Street and the boards were built in Sunshine Beach. At one point, I got a call late one night from the public bar of the Casino Hotel saying Kevin wanted to talk to me. They put him on and his voice was raspy – he was obviously still smoking. He sounded drunk, but I could tell it was him and was pleased to hear his voice. It had been many years since we had spoken.

He wanted me to send him some pictures so he could prove to his kids that he was a surfer. The next day I went through my files and cut out a couple of pics from magazines, then sent them off to the address he'd given me. Unfortunately, that was the last I heard of Platty. A few months later he died – another beautiful surfer gone before his time. He was only fifty-six.

Bob Evans was my mentor – my dad in more ways than my biological father was. My take on why he sort of adopted me was because he had married a much younger woman and had three young children, and I guess I was in the right age bracket to be the son/ mate with whom he could go up and down the coast chasing waves.

Our friendship started during my formative years. In 1961, I was thirteen. Apparently Evo had watched me surfing my home break at Collaroy and could see potential. I remember vividly the day we met. I was attending Narrabeen Boys High School and it was a day just like any other. I burst through the back door of our house and went to fling my schoolbag and there was Bob Evans, having a cup of tea with my mum and asking her if I could go on a surfari up the coast with him. My mum was totally charmed by Bob. He was a real gentleman, a suave ladies' man.

I don't know what year it was when Bob got his colostomy bag. He never mentioned it to me. I think I found out from Jean Platt, who, as I mentioned, used to make all our board shorts back then. I asked her why she was making Bob's boardies with such a high waist. It was so out of fashion – we all wore our shorts hanging off our hips. Then I found out it was to hide his bag.

Bob was a competent surfer but we only paddled out together a few times over all those years because he was always shooting movie footage. Back in the 16-foot (4.9-metre) wooden 'toothpick' era, he earned the nickname 'Serge' after taking off behind a particular nasty 'surge rock' halfway along the point break at Fairy Bower, on Sydney's north side. He told me about going to Torquay for the 1956 surf carnival associated with the Olympic Games. He managed to buy Greg Noll's malibu board, which was the beginning of a love affair that lasted all his life.

On the way back home from one of those early trips, Bob asked me what I wanted to do with my life. I said I wanted to leave school and surf. I was good with tools, liked getting my hands dirty with resin and foam, had had a go at reshaping an old balsa board, and had been fixing dings for a year or two. He said he knew one of Australia's biggest surfboard makers, Gordon Woods, very well and would talk to him about getting me a shaping apprenticeship.

Bob mentioned my name to Gordon, and that was how he came to Collaroy to see me surf. For the next couple of years I was completely happy learning the trade, living at home, hanging out in Collaroy with my mates, and going away with Evo whenever he said go.

When the first surf craze hit Australia, Evo was the man on the spot: Mr Surf in Sydney. He was writing a weekly column for the *Sunday Telegraph* newspaper, which was owned by one of Australia's richest men, Sir Frank Packer. Through this contact, he organised sponsorship for the 1963 Invitational Australian Championships at Bondi. The prize was a first-class airfare to America, and I won.

Bob then began to play an even bigger role in my life. Somewhere along the line he had met and become quite friendly with one of our most famous cricketers, Richie Benaud. Alongside Don Bradman, Benaud was Australian cricketing royalty. By the mid-'6os, he had retired from playing cricket but was making big money doing commentary. He was also writing books and had a daily newspaper column that was syndicated around the world.

Bob set up a meeting for me with Richie to get some advice. Richie lived with his wife, Daphne, in a cluttered unit in Coogee in the eastern suburbs of Sydney. They ran his whole business from their unit. He explained what I needed to do to make a business out of being a sports star. Write some books, he said – a how-to first, then the history of your sport, and one day an autobiography. He asked me if I could write and I explained that I had left school at fifteen and had no idea. He said that wasn't a problem. They would get a 'ghostie' to write my newspaper column for a few months. He made a call or two while I had a cuppa with Daphne, and that was how I ended up writing a weekly column for Packer's *Sunday Telegraph* for the next nine years.

My editor at the *Tele* was Frank Margan, another friend of Bob's, who was one of the doyens of the Australian wine industry. I met him at a Thursday wine-tasting luncheon, and he helped a great deal with my column.

Bob loved Hawaii, especially Waikiki. The surf, the beach boys, the palm trees on the beach, the big hotels with tropical bars and gorgeous girls. For him, Waikiki was a magical place that encapsulated everything he loved about Hawaii. He would plan his whole day around the cocktail hour. In those days, the roads on Oahu weren't crowded and parking was easy, close to the beach in the city. We would drive in from the country on many afternoons just in time to watch the sunset from the beachside bar of the Royal Hawaiian Hotel. Evo lived for sitting there, staring at the horizon, searching for the elusive green flash while sucking on a mai tai, listening to Arthur Lyman singing 'Yellow Bird'.

Bob was friends with another photographer, Bud Brown, and they were like-minded spirits in many ways – both passionate about shooting movies of surfing. One day, they decided we would go to Maui. No one other than the locals knew much about the island's mysterious Honolua Bay. Bud figured out how to get there, so he was the guide, and John Peck from California was the other invited surfer. The waves were fantastic, with no one out, as Bud's and Bob's movies show.

After I got my Australian driver's licence in 1964, everything changed for me. About once a week, Evo invited me to come have lunch with him and different prospective sponsors. Downtown Sydney was so innocent in the '60s. You could park anywhere, have a little too much to drink, drive home and not get arrested.

Lunch was always at places like French's Tavern and other upmarket Sydney restaurants. Bob taught me how to dress: he took me to buy my first custom-made suit. The whole experience was fantastic. In the process of hanging out with him, I learnt a lot about how the Sydney business world turned. I got to meet the executives of many of Australia's biggest companies, including the promotions manager of Ampol Petroleum, Terry Southwell-Keely. Ampol had sponsored the first World Championship at Manly in 1964, and Bob's energy and contacts had made that event happen.

Evo taught me never to talk business at lunch – that was bad manners while you were eating. He told me to just enjoy the company unless the other party was inclined to discuss advertising, which they invariably did, primed with a good Aussie red. Evo's policy was to always put your best foot forward, and always go and buy a new tie if there was a really important deal on the table.

In September of 1962, he published the first issue of *Surfing World* magazine. As anyone who has been in the magazine business knows, survival relies on editorial and advertising, not necessarily in that order. He collected the material for the mag from personal experiences and contacts. There were lots of stories on our trips up the coast.

As far as advertising went, Evo was a super salesman, softly spoken and smooth as silk. His business partner was a big, burly ex-detective named Jack Keegan. I don't know how long they were in business together – I don't even know if Jack had any ties to the surf. I only met him a few times. I remember the match between them always seemed strange to me.

The magazine's offices were in a colourful part of Sydney down near Chinatown – lots of hookers, plus the markets, the railways and cheap ethnic restaurants. A bit later, Evans and Keegan started a men's mag called *Squire*, which was edited by a funny little man named Jack de Lissa. By this stage, Evo had a pretty heavy workload. Selling advertising for *Surfing World* was his primary job, but running up the coast to get editorial content and shoot movie footage was also super important. Somehow, he made time to write his column for the *Sunday Telegraph*.

Over lunch with a friend of his who was the number one radio personality in the city, he dreamt up the idea of doing a surf report. It was the first in Australia and he convinced radio station 2SM to put in a landline from the station to his home in Elanora, right behind Narrabeen. He told me he saw his surf reports as good money for checking the surf and talking about it, and that's what he did every day, regardless. The thing was, Bob filled up every waking minute. He was working his arse off, leaving little time for his family.

On many weekends, Bob and his wife, Valerie, plus John Witzig and I, would have Sunday lunch in the beautiful old terrace house in Bondi Junction belonging to Jackie and Ross Kelly. Ross was a talented Bondi surfer from the same era as Evo. He was good-looking and an executive for Rothmans, the huge tobacco company. Jackie was an ex-model who loved to entertain.

At one memorable lunch, I recall the entire conversation consisted of a discussion about Witzig taking over the helm at *Surfing World*. This was around July 1966, the outset of 'the New Era'. Bob understood that surfing was headed in a different direction, one that he could only sit back and watch, so he made John the editor. He never actually took his name off the magazine as editor but in fact John produced the entire magazine. At some point, a well-heeled Englishman named Gareth Powell entered the scene and tried to buy *SW* but Evo declined, as it was the promotional vehicle for his films. Instead, Gareth bought Witzig and started his own surf mag, *Surf International*, and a girlie mag called *Chance*.

Around this time, I started to drift away from Evo. Perhaps it was the pot I was smoking, or the back-to-nature lifestyle I was living. I got married, left Sydney and moved to Byron Bay in 1969. Evo was not against pot as such. I recall he had a puff on a joint at the Kellys' house after lunch one Sunday. He remarked that booze was his preferred drug and that was the end of it.

We were all cool with that. Valerie had a more open approach and said she didn't mind a bit of both. I am not sure of the details, but their marriage fell apart officially in 1969. I know he had not been in love with her for a long time and had fallen for a younger woman named Ingrid, who I met on his arm at a surfing do in the mid-'70s.

Evo died in a hotel room in Jacksonville, Florida, in 1975. He was only forty-seven years old. The official cause of death was a massive brain haemorrhage. Thinking back on this, I can understand how it could happen, as he was not very disciplined about taking his blood-pressure pills. Exactly what he was doing in America at the time was confusing to many of us. Basically, he was working for a company that found compatible partners in the US and Australia – Evo would broker the deal between the two parties. The job provided a good steady income, and Evo's softspoken charm meant that he was well suited to the work.

I still think back fondly to those days from time to time, with Evo, Val, the Kellys and John Witzig. I am reminded of one of the songs we used to listen to – 'Bob Dylan's Dream'.

Bobby Brown and me looking over Greenmount – a still taken from Bob Evans' movie, *The Young Wave Hunters*. **Evans family**

6

EDGE BOARDS

Right from my first peek at the tiny red spaceship tucked under Bunker Spreckels' arm, I had my suspicions about the board he was holding. The 5 foot 6 inch (1.7 metre) looked weird – super-low rails, handles embedded in the top of each rail, 10-centimetres thick, its girth carrying all the way to the tail with almost no lift. I figured it was some kind of bizarre kneeboard. Interesting, but not my cup of tea.

Bunker surfed it both ways – standing up and on his knees. The handles were for steering deep in the tube. Later that afternoon, I saw him riding the board at Tunnels on Kauai, one of the hollowest right-hand tubes I have ever seen. It was a perfect day, waves 4 to 5 feet (1.2 to 1.5 metres), glassy, not a drop of water out of place.

When Bunker paddled out, I remember thinking the board

looked too short. He was almost fully submerged and I couldn't imagine he would ever catch a wave. Then he took off deep, pulling himself to his feet at the last minute and emerging right out of the wave face. He was way behind the curl as he pulled in. He disappeared inside the curtain, exiting a few seconds later at lightning speed.

Bunker Spreckels with his down-rail 'Alma' board, built by Bob Smith on Clark Gable's ranch in Encino, California, in mid-1968. *Art Brewer*

The keel fin on Bunker's 'Alma' board. *Art Brewer*

That was almost fifty years ago. For a good portion of those years, I have wondered about the lineage of that design – Bunker's was the first low-railed board I'd ever seen. Who were the pioneers of this breakthrough, which I've always considered such a significant part of the so-called shortboard revolution? My research has turned up some hidden treasures, a whole bunch of stuff that I had no idea about until I started asking questions and correlating the answers. As with many breakthroughs, there was more than one person at the design's core.

Rewinding a bit to the shortboard revolution itself, it's easy to get into an argument over the origins of the board. Some old surfers believe it was McTavish and me in Australia. Others believe it was Brewer, Reno Abellira and Lopez in Hawaii. I happen to know the 'shortboard revolution' quite well. I was one of the few surfers in the world with sponsorship in the 1960s; the only other Australian was Keith Paull. This freedom allowed me to move from Australia to America via Hawaii every few months. In transit, I saw a lot of experimentation.

I believe there was a genuine desire to ride deeper in the curl at the time, and this quest brought the shortboard into existence in Australia and Hawaii simultaneously. I don't believe there was any conscious copying of other shapers' designs. Everywhere I travelled during that era, I would hear stories of surfers cutting down their longboards. In France, Australia, England, America, South Africa, surfers were cutting centimetres off the length, sometimes more than 30-centimetres in one hack.

We were living in a very experimental period. Drugs were new and exciting. Everyone was making boards in their backyard. Drop out, tune in – this was the anthem of the late '60s and early '70s. As shapers, we were searching for more sensitive equipment with every fresh blank we attacked. A lot of people found the keys simultaneously. As such, synchronicity played a huge role in the shortboard's evolution and I believe it was the same with low-rail boards, or edge boards as they've come to be known.

The first surfboard with a chine, or edges, that I saw was one of George Greenough's hulls. I remember George saying it needed perfect waves to work; then he went back to tinkering with the design, sanding the chine off the bottom.

Until recently, I believed that Bunker's edge board with the handles, on Kauai, had been shaped by a surfer named Vinny Bryan. That was not correct – a shaper named Bob Smith had designed, shaped, glassed, sanded and wet-rubbed it. When we spoke a few years ago, Smith confirmed he had made that board. It was nicknamed 'Alma' and was built on the Gable ranch in Encino, California in mid-December 1968. Apparently Bunker's stepfather, Clark Gable, was delighted to have the boys building boards on his ranch.

Smith is an interesting character. An inventor, he currently holds two US patents – one for a high-speed sailboat that he believes could go faster than Paul Larsen's 65-knot, world-record boat, and the other for a locking electrical plug. I'm not sure how the two are connected, but that's how his mind works. He told me he would apply for many more patents if his finances allowed it.

Everyone who knows the backstory of edge boards largely considers Smith to be the father of the design. His real name is Robert Imhoff. He was born in Michigan and raised in California, a goofy-foot originally, then a switchfoot from 1968 onward. He's also a long-time devotee of Scientology.

When he was young, he made a couple of traditional tankers in his family garage in South Pasadena. For one reason or another,

he changed his name from Imhoff to Smith in 1967 and moved to
the North Shore of Oahu. He's a bit reluctant to divulge exactly
why he changed his handle, though I figure it must have been the
Vietnam War draft. He says the short answer is 'You can't drop
out if you take everything with you.' It makes sense when you
think about it.

Just like hundreds of surfers with their ear to the underground,
Bob cut a foot (30-centimetres) off his last longboard during this
period. He ended up with a sweet 9 foot 4 inch (2.8 metre) that was
pretty thin with traditional rails. Bob had to be fit to paddle that
board, as it floated very low in the water. It sounded a lot like my
board 'Sam', and they had almost the same dimensions (there is a
whole chapter on Sam in my autobiography, *Nat's Nat and That's
That*). After this came an 8-foot (2.4-metre) semi-gun, also with
standard high/low rails, then a 7 foot (2.1-metre) using the same
basic design. By the beginning of the summer of 1968, Bob's boards
were down to 6 feet 8 inches (2 metres) with full down rails.

In December 1968, on the North Shore, I had the chance to
ride a few waves on Bob's 6-foot 8-inch edge board. I recall that it
was extremely fast and manoeuvrable. I could hardly keep it in the
water. Bunker's 5-foot 6-inch (1.7-metre) Alma board was a shorter
version of Bob's 6 foot 8 inch. Bob was always trying to get more
speed, power and manoeuvrability from his surfboards. The trick
was to get really good acceleration out of a turn. His 6 foot 8 inch
was 20 inches (50 centimetres) wide and 27 inches (68 centimetres)
back from the nose with a broad vee in the front end. He noticed
that if he buried the rail all the way to the nose in an attempt to
make a long section, the surfboard would slow down. The lack of
belly in the nose enabled him to keep the same rocker. Where the
vee met the rails Bob made a hard edge, giving the board hard rails

nose-to-tail, which was a huge success in terms of performance. It was loose and quick, on the verge of spinning out half the time.

The low rail eliminated the problem of the board slowing down out of a turn. Bob could now bury the rail to the tip of the nose and accelerate. He and his friends were looking for more challenging waves without crowds to share them with, so they started riding the rights at Pipeline in the spring of 1968. They were the only ones out there until December, when Bunker showed up. According to Bob, Bunker rode 'hand-me-down' edge boards through that winter. The first board Bob recalls making for Bunker was the Alma. It was the last board he made with a vee in the nose. The vee served no useful purpose, he told me, except to transition from belly to flat bottom – flat from edge to edge, with rocker nose-to-tail.

Later, Bob made a board for another surfer, Rick Value. Rick had drawn a template and wanted Bob to shape the design. Bob refused, telling him he wouldn't like it, but Rick kept pestering him so he made it. The board didn't work for Rick, as predicted, but Bunker liked it and bought it from him.

Bob was meeting a lot of other surfers on the North Shore, including a talented local natural-foot named Vinny Bryan. Vinny was born in Florida in 1944 and his family moved to Ewa Beach, on Oahu, when he was two years old. His dad was in the military service when they moved to Hawaii and eventually became a manager for the Ewa Sugar Plantation.

Vinny's dad surfed a bit and introduced his son to wave riding when he was three years old. He was a tall, lanky kid, keen to have a go at anything related to the ocean. He started shaping his own boards in his dad's garage.

In 1965, he married a Californian girl named Alice and they both attended college in San Luis Obispo. Like so many other

young people in the late '6os, Alice and Vinny were searching for
spiritual enlightenment. The true path for them was the Bahá'í
faith, which teaches the value and worth of all religions and the
unity and equality of all people. Its origins are in Persia, but it's an
independent worldwide religion.

Alice had three kids in the space of ten years and Vinny endeavoured to continue his involvement with surfing. With a friend, he
opened Central Coast Surf Shop, the only shop selling surfboards
for hundreds of kilometres around. Vinny shaped, glassed and finished all the boards in his garage. He did not like the chemicals
associated with glassing, but it was the only way to get the boards
finished.

After the family moved back to Hawaii, Vinny would leave
the shaped blanks for Bob Smith to glass and finish. By then, he
was already an extremely competent surfer. Unfortunately, his
surfing had to take a back seat so he could pay the rent and feed
his growing family.

The move back to the islands encouraged them to become
even more serious Bahá'í practitioners; however, Vinny's faith was
evolving. He often returned to Bahá'í principles while embracing
his own spiritual understanding, which revolved around surfing.
Vinny was in his prime, regarded by his peers as a strong family
man and one of the best underground surfers on the North Shore.

After meeting Bob Smith, he shaped a 7 foot 6 inch (2.3 metre)
with a belly in the nose. After trying it, he commented to Bob that
it was slow coming out of a driving forehand turn. Vinny told
Bob he intended to shape a board with a vee in the nose like a
boat. The next week he did just that and the board addressed the
bogging-down in forehand turns, which led the way to the rails
going lower and harder all the way around.

Independently, Vinny and Bob had reached the same conclusion about the hard edges. The pair surfed Ala Moana a lot that summer of 1968. 'I never made a board for Vinny, nor Vinny for me,' Bob adamantly pointed out when we spoke a few years ago, 'but Vinny did try some of my boards on occasion. One of the best rides I saw Vinny get was on that first edge board at Off the Wall, not long after I made it. He had an incredible amount of speed and was very far back in the tube.'

The next board Vinny made for himself was an asymmetrical. He won a contest at Honolua Bay on Maui on that board. Naturally it had edges. Everyone who was on the cliffs that day in the winter of 1968 stood in awe as Vinny carved all over the face of Honolua's walls. He managed to find the best waves in the perfect 6-foot (1.8-metre) surf, gaining the upper hand over the hottest Hawaiian surfer in the world at that time, Jock Sutherland. Jock finished second riding a traditional longboard.

Vinny and Alice split up in 1974 and he married another Haole girl, Christine, in 1981. She had three kids from a previous marriage and Vinny stepped up to become their dad. It must have been an action-packed family scene, especially with Alice and her new husband living in the same neighbourhood on Kauai and all six kids moving back and forth from one house to the other.

Both homes were full of love and good music. If you talk to local people on Kauai, they will say they loved Vinny for the way he played twelve-string, slack-key guitar in the traditional Hawaiian style. Right up until his death, in June 2015, Vinny was a well-respected elder of the Hanalei community. The fact that he was a world-class surfer who comfortably won the only contest he ever entered was a sidebar.

*

Dana Nicely, the first surfer to bring a down-rail edge board to Australia, 1969. *Art Brewer*

Dana driving down the line at Rocky Point on that same little disc. *Art Brewer*

Alongside Vinny and Bob Smith, the list of test pilots for the earli-
est edge boards includes Rick Value, Todd Value, Douglas Gross,
Eric Gross, Robbie Bushnei, Brian Kennelly and Dana Nicely.
Bunker was not a part of the original crew, though he eventually
became involved. I have not been able to track down the Gross
brothers and Robbie Bushnei, but the other four were open to talk
about their edge-board experiences.

Dana Nicely is still living in Kauai, playing music and fully
committed to surfing. He was born in 1947, also into a military
family. The family were stationed in Greece when the Second
World War ended and eventually moved back to Oahu so Dana
and his three brothers could get a traditional education. He ended
up attending Punahou School, where he became friendly with
Vinny Bryan. Punahou was a hotbed of surfers in the 1960s: Ricky

Grigg, Peter Cole and Fred Van Dyke were all teachers, and Jeff Hakman and Gerry Lopez were students a year behind Dana.

When Dana graduated in 1970, he took off for Australia with his edge board under his arm. He was a quality surfer and shaper who left his mark in the land of Oz, spending six months travelling the east coast from Byron Bay to Victoria. He turned up at the 1970 World Championship like a breath of offshore wind, always keen to go surfing, singing the praises of edge boards to anyone who was interested. I'd met Dana in Byron Bay when he first arrived in Oz. There were quite a few travelling Americans cruising in our town in that period. Some were on the run from the draft, others were just out for any good adventure. Certainly, there were too many to get to know everyone well. When Dana and I talked at the beach, he struck me as a really nice guy – a smooth seppo who surfed well and had a knack of always turning up at just the right time on our fickle point breaks around Byron.

As for the rest of the crew, Brian Kennelly moved to Oahu in 1967. He met Bob Smith there and rode kneeboards and stand-up boards with Bob and Bunker at every beach on the 11-kilometre stretch of the North Shore. The Value brothers moved from their childhood home, which was close to Honolulu, to the North Shore about a year later.

Then, in the summer of 1969, most of the edge pilots rented a big red house in Mokuleia, out towards Kaena Point, past Haleiwa. They turned the garage into a workshop. All of them either shaped their own boards or glassed them. They obsessed over the edges and the bottoms of their boards and hand-shaped thick, foiled fins out of foam. They also developed their own removable fin system featuring a dovetail joint between the fin and the box, where you'd drive the fin home and hold it with a pin.

There was a lot of experimentation in every facet of board building. Brian lived a half-block down the road. He said that every day he went over to the red house, they were as busy as beavers, shaping, sanding and glassing. It was a hive of activity.

In order to save money, Bunker and Rick Value moved into Rick's car. A few days later, they found an abandoned army bunker above Pipeline near the old Bummer Hill road, and lived in the cold concrete pillbox with centipedes and cane spiders for a couple of months. Bunker's mother, Kay Spreckels Gable, heir to the Spreckels and Gable fortunes, did not approve of Bunker becoming a surf bum and cut him off financially to teach him a lesson. Naturally, she had no idea about the groundbreaking developments in surfboard design that the boys were working on. Either way, when Bunker explained the situation to her, she wired a good chunk of cash. Bunker really loved his mum, and the feeling was mutual.

Clearly, Bob Smith and Vinny were the main visionaries and shapers, backed up by the Value brothers. As is the case in the rest of the surfing world, it was the kneeboarders who pushed the limits of extreme shortboards from 1967 through 1969. Vinny said that the size and design of the boards were a necessity. He wanted to ride uncrowned spots like Rocky Rights and Backdoor Pipeline. He needed to go fast, which pushed the experimentation. Bob Smith, Brian, Vinny and Bunker were the first surfers to ride Backdoor consistently. Up to that point, no one thought you could go right at Pipeline.

When I met him on Kauai, Vinny was keen to point out that a lot of the experimentation with their surfboards took place under the influence of LSD – they did it as a group, often combining it with intense yoga and always including heavy surf sessions. Most of it took place on waves that no one had dreamt could be surfed. He also maintained that even without acid, he was sure they would have reached the same place, but the experiment benefited from the drug.

Bob stayed on the mainland during the summer of 1969 and moved back to the North Shore in September. Vinny remained with Bunker and made a 5-foot 6-inch (1.7-metre) egg, which was the board he took to Kauai when he and Bunker went over in the autumn. From that board, he sorted out fin templates for stability and power.

Bob soon joined them. Like many other surfers on the North Shore, they were looking to the outer islands since Oahu was getting too crowded. The north shore of Kauai sounded like it had all the answers. They moved over and stayed with Tommy Chamberlain first, asking him where the hollowest, fastest waves were. He told them to check Tunnels but warned that no one rode there much – it was too shallow and the reef was dry at the end.

They had it mostly to themselves. The pair left Kauai in December 1969: Bunker had to go home for a family Christmas in California and Bob had to return to Oahu to continue his Scientology studies. Bunker was clearly looking for some direction and went with Bob to the Church of Scientology on Oahu. Unfortunately, he never caught on to what it was about. Perhaps if he had hung with Bob more and had not inherited such a big pile of cash, he would still be with us today. Bob is adamant that drugs and Scientology do not mix.

In August 1970, Bunker inherited millions from the Spreckels family fortune and had to travel back to Los Angeles to sign all the papers. Prior to this, he was enrolled in California Western University in San Diego for a short time. In between classes, he and Brian Kennelly became close friends, spending more time hunting waves in the Sunset Cliffs area than going to campus. Naturally, Bunker had an edge board with him. They hooked up with a much younger pair of surfers, Ben Ferris and Jon Riddle, who were two stoked local kids from Newbreak. Both of these groms were already into shaping and riding their own boards. Instantly, they saw the benefit of the hard down rails and followed Bunker back to Hawaii.

When Bunker returned to the islands, he moved into a spacious house at Wainiha, near Tunnels on the north shore of Kauai. The elevated living and sleeping areas were about 3 metres off the ground. Underneath them, they installed a complete surfboard factory – everything from a shaping room to a glassing and polishing area. It was a big playground, just for him and his friends.

Bunker provided as many blanks and as much resin and glass as the boys desired, and they were in heaven. Word is that shaping legends Dick Brewer and Mike Diffenderfer shaped a few of their beautiful semi-guns there. Even Gerry Lopez passed through. The master of the San Diego fish, Steve Lis, made a trip to Kauai and met up with Vinny Bryan. After they surfed together and compared notes, the conclusion was that edge boards really were a definite design breakthrough that demonstrated the potential of top speed. The only issue was that they had problems with handling. They worked well in perfect waves when ridden by talented surfers, but they weren't for everyone.

Bob made a board for Bunker at the Wainiha house in 1970. He was on a weekend break from his religious studies on Oahu and it was one of the few times he experimented with a board for

someone else. Usually he experimented with his own board, and
when he was satisfied with the results, would make a similar one
for someone else.

Anyway, Bob made that one for Bunker, then soon thereafter
made another one just like it for himself. It rode okay in good
waves but was too extreme. Bob could tell Bunker didn't like
his – it magnified those handling problems he'd been having. Bob's
was a great board to learn from, but he's always maintained that
edge boards are very critical and not at all forgiving.

Around this time, Bunker invited Rick and Todd Value to come
over from Oahu to stay with him, Ferris and Riddle at Wainiha.
The Value brothers were quality surfers who had been shaping
their own boards since high school. In the fall of 1969 Brian
Kennelly also moved to Kauai, staying at Bunker's for a short time
along with another close friend, the talented shaper and surfer
Bill Hamilton. In order to fuel their surfing habits, they started
working as busboys at the Anchorage. Brian was a waiter there,
which meant he got a cut of the tips.

The house at Tunnels was a perfect environment for further
experimentation with surfboard design. Everyone living there was
a dedicated disciple of edge boards. The house was like an artists'
bordello – something you could imagine Michelangelo and other
artists being a part of in Florence during the High Renaissance.

Vinny, Rick, Todd, Jon and Ben were all experienced and talented shapers, and they were all making their own boards. But the
inspiration and direction for the edge rail came directly from Bob
Smith. The test wave for the design was Tunnels. On any given
day, with any sort of wave, they were out there. Bunker decided
to have each of the boys make boards for him. Finally, they all
told him to do one for himself. Bunker spent days and days in the

shaping room chipping away at the blank in order to get exactly
what he wanted. Then he completed the glassing and sanding
himself. He did all the dirty work, just to prove that he could.
When it was finally finished, he took it out and ripped.

The place was obviously a hotbed of innovation. But as I mentioned earlier, the shortboard revolution was diffused and there
were a lot of people coming to similar conclusions at the same
time. A totally different take on the origins of edge boards and
down rails involves Mike Hynson. I have been a long-time admirer
of Mike. With all that slicked-back long blond hair, he added up
to the classic, prototypical California surfer. He looked unques-
tionably cool travelling around the world in the first *Endless
Summer*. I guess I identified with his role in the movie more than
Robert August's. Don't get me wrong – I thought they were both
great, but as totally different characters they played off each other,
which was the reason Bruce Brown chose them.

I got to know Hynson pretty well over the years. After we
became friends, he told me about his little pipe and the secret
stash he kept camouflaged in his board bag for the whole twelve
months he was on the road for *The Endless Summer*. He was
getting stoned the whole time, which was a little ahead of the
curve for 1962.

In the late '70s, we were hanging out at his old house on High
Street in La Jolla with his beautiful wife, Melinda. Michael is a
great talker. Over the many years of our friendship, he's told me
the story I relate here more than once, but that was the first time I
heard it.

As he tells it, one day in the summer of 1967, he was surfing
Mala Wharf on Maui, crouched down nice and low in a backside

squat. Pretty soon the board spun out and the arse end flew around, and Hynson found himself still standing on the board with the tail forward. Since the wave still had open face, he steered back up into the curl and continued turning down the line until the wave dissipated.

He was riding a traditional board for the day, with high rails in the front and normal hard low rails in the tail. When he reached the beach, his overwhelming revelation was that the board rode better with the low rails forward: it was faster and more responsive. And that was the last time Mike made a board with traditional rails. Every board he shaped after that had low rails all the way around.

Herbie Fletcher has confirmed this scenario, and all of Hynson's team riders got on low railers within a few weeks. They all embraced the feeling. The Hynson team was impressive and included Les Potts and the talented David Nuuhiwa. I should add that Herbie also says he saw an old black-and-white photo of a down railer made by Joe Quigg in the '50s, but unfortunately I cannot find that picture.

In November 1969, Wayne Lynch, Ted Spencer, Paul Witzig and I rented a house just down the road from Bunker's, in front of Tunnels. We were working on a movie called *Sea of Joy*. After that aforementioned first glimpse of Bunker, I was fascinated, and ended up hanging out with him at every opportunity. Part of the attraction, I'm sure, was the pillowcase he had that was half full of peyote buttons. We digested the tea on many mornings before going surfing.

Even without the drugs, Bunker looked like a cosmic space child with his basin-cut, blond, Greenough-style hair. He was also intense. He had some great one-liners – sarcastic, off-the-cuff comments that instantly made you either love him or hate him.

A season or two later, after he had inherited his money from Clark Gable and his mum, I bumped into Bunker out in the surf on the North Shore of Oahu. He said he wanted me to have dinner with him at an upmarket restaurant called the Crouching Lion in Kahuku. Later that evening, he sent a driver to pick me up. I recall that we had a nice dinner and talked about the movie he wanted to make about his life. His driver drove me back to the North Shore and the evening was all pretty uneventful. Bunker was really mellow that night. I knew that he could be over the top sometimes, but he seemed quite normal to me. That was the last time I saw my friend Bunker Spreckels.

Going back to my stay on Kauai in 1969, I was keen to get home afterwards and shape edge rails into my next board. When I arrived in Sydney, I had one thing on my mind: to get into the shaping room at Keyo Surfboards in Brookvale. Once I was set up, I made a longer version of what Bob Smith and the crew were riding in Kauai. The first one was 7 feet (2.1 metres) by 21 inches (53 centimetres), with a soft square tail. I surfed that board in beach break on the Northern Beaches of Sydney. It was super-sensitive, not forgiving at all, but fast. The rails were almost knife-edged. I glassed the deck first, taking a razor blade to zip off the jellied glass before finishing the bottom.

During the next few months, I made several of these boards and they got smaller and smaller in length, stopping at 5 feet 10 inches (1.8 metres). I won the 1970 New South Wales state titles at Narrabeen on that last board. It was fantastic. In addition to being slightly shorter than me, it had softened rails. I used a hard pad to shape a more forgiving rail, tucking the edge further back under the bottom of the board. This slight change stopped it from biting in a turn and throwing you off with the sudden movement. McTavish had shaped one with a tucked-under edge earlier, and he turned me on to this subtlety. The tweak fixed the problem of having to ride on the bottom of the wave and catch the rail when you least expected it.

As further proof that kneeboarders were instrumental in the down-rail design, I recall that Greenough persisted with the chine or edge theory. In Victoria in 1970, he built a black-railed spoon with a quarter-inch (6 millimetre) chine where the rail joined the bottom. I watched him surf that board at solid 8-foot (2.4-metre) Winkipop and it was fantastic. When he gravitated to windsurfing, George said he really felt the benefit of the chine. The Greenough boards were very stable at high speed. Recently, he has followed that same theory into a series of surfboards he built for Dave Rastovich to take to Fiji. Apparently Rasta was impressed with the handling and speed.

Back in 1969, the benefits of low rails spread around surfing like a wildfire. Every shaper in the world was trying low rails and every top surfer I knew was discovering the benefits of this style of design. Rail shapes have not changed much since.

7

DONALD AND DEWEY

Donald Takayama was the embodiment of the aloha spirit. He was the essence of exactly what being a surfer should be. He was committed to spreading that vibe, no matter what nationality, colour, creed or sex you are.

Donald grew up in Waikiki and began surfing at the age of seven. In 1957, when he was about thirteen, he saved his paper-route money and moved to California, where he scored a shaping job with Velzy-Jacobs Surfboards in Venice Beach. When the business broke up he threw in his lot with Hap Jacobs, shaping boards and using the money to indulge in hotting up cars. Later, wishing to stay in the South Bay area of LA, he moved to Bing Surfboards, shaping the classic noserider that David Nuuhiwa rode to prominence in the mid-1960s.

When Dewey Weber became *the* surfboard to have in California, Donald joined the team. Under the watchful eye of fellow Hawaiian and head shaper Harold Iggy, he went on to become the most sought-after shaper in Dewey's prestigious stable. Then, after twenty years of dedication, Donald became the most respected and prolific longboard shaper in the world. Every longboard surfer at some time has owned, or wished they owned, a Takayama.

The actual design of Donald's boards evolved over fifty years. Originally, he tested them all personally. An explosive little goofy-foot, he was such a fine surfer that he could feel every minor variation underfoot and then intentionally enhance or nullify that variation in his next board.

His competitive record is impressive: three USA Championships, in 1971, 1972 and 1973. In the 1990s he won a couple more US titles, but these achievements offer only a passing insight into what a fine surfer he was.

Donald moved to North County in San Diego in 1969 and started his own surfboard company, Hawaiian Pro Designs. Unfortunately, spending so much time in the shaping bay meant less time surfing. As HPD's surf team grew, Donald oversaw the manufacture of hundreds of boards for his riders, personally checking every surfer's feelings about the performance of his latest creation. Depending on the surfer, he would soften the rail in the tail or make the edge harder where the bottom-shape joined the rail. Donald's boards never had much lift – keeping the nose close to the water was critical – which meant they worked best in smaller waves. On the other hand, a quality surfer could make them work in anything.

Donald's wife, Sydney Diane, ran the office. It was crazy – some people were willing to wait up to a year for a personally shaped

Takayama longboard. Donald obviously worked hard and tried out other shapers, but no one had his touch. Eventually he teamed up with Tommy Moss, but they still couldn't keep up with the orders. The Thailand-based manufacturer Surftech, which has produced thousands of HPD boards, filled the void. That may have solved the problem of production, but Donald still insisted that he shape every team rider's board personally.

Donald Takayama, surfing strong into his twilight years. *Kevin Kinnear*

Donald and Syd Takayama. *Kevin Kinnear*

I've always thought of all my Donald-shaped longboards as being like Cadillacs. They deliver a long, smooth ride. You just slip them into drive and cruise on the freeway at 160 kilometres an hour.

The first board I ever received from Donald simply arrived one day, for my fortieth birthday. After that, every decade he would shape and send me a new longboard from halfway around the world. It was a complete surprise each time. The first two were classic Takayama/Nat Young hybrids with paisley material on the deck. I rode them both into the ground. For my sixtieth, another one turned up in Australia; this time, it was a pure Takayama longboard. I guess by then I half expected it. Still, once I saw it, I decided I'd never surf it. It was a work of art by a master crafts-man. He had spent months shaving away the balsa, honing the contrasting dark cedar stringers, meticulously manicuring every detail. He personally glued up the tail block to match the dark and light contrasts in the board and laminated the timber in the fin, carefully hand-sanding the resin bead. The board hangs over my desk at my farm in Australia and is now an heirloom, to be kept in our family forever.

When he was still alive, it took me a while to get used to being woken up by Donald at 5 a.m. California time regardless of wher-ever I happened to be in the world. It occurred so often over the course of thirty years that it became a ritual. He would call full of cheer just after he'd finished shaping. He worked on a similar clock as mine, but he was extreme. I mean, we were both early risers, but Donald was almost nocturnal.

After his daily shaping sessions, which ran from midnight until 4 a.m., he would make a few calls. I imagine these chats took hours, and I'm sure I wasn't the only friend he woke up. He could talk the leg off a chair. At one point, while my wife and

I were staying in Sydney with my mother-in-law, Veda became so used to his morning bell that she actually looked forward to her little chats with him. She complained the first few times but in the end she dearly missed Donald's voice when we moved away.

Donald always called for my birthday, as I did for his. We were both Scorpios and understood the good and bad aspects of our natures. He sure was a lucky little bugger. He would tell me stories about winning huge bets at a Native American casino just inland from his Oceanside shop. Apparently he won enough once to buy Syd a new top-of-the-line Mercedes. I was amazed.

In passing, I mentioned that I'd like to go to that casino one day. Then, on one of my trips to California a few years later, Syd, Donald and I made up a war party. Right from the moment we entered the place, Donald was treated like royalty. The management loved him – which I had a hard time understanding, given that he had taken so much of their loot over the years, until he explained to me that he regularly brought Japanese businessmen in with him who lost heaps.

Donald loved the pokies. That day he won buckets of money, running five machines simultaneously. They all overflowed within the first few minutes. He gave me a full bucket and asked me to help him out. I told him I had never gambled much, but he said I had to help him – he couldn't keep up.

I lost the lot quick smart, so he gave me another bucket of coins. We had a great day. He also did this to me in Costa Rica. I was on my way to surf early one morning when I heard bells ringing and saw lights flashing and people running around inside the casino where we were staying. Donald stuck his head out from the crowd, gave me a bucket of coins and yelled at me, 'They're hungry today, Nat. Help me feed the buggers!'

I never knew Donald to have a drink. He was a teetotaller for all our years together. Did not touch a drop – didn't need it. He was really funny without booze, a happy Hawaiian who loved to see his friends having a good time.

On one promotional trip to Japan, we were staying at a very traditional hotel with a handful of other guys. We had a nice Japanese dinner, and one big bottle of sake turned into too many. Even though he wasn't drinking, Donald invented a move called the Drop Knee Sake, which entailed sculling a full glass of rice wine while going through all the positions of a drop knee turn. It was just like riding a wave. We all had our own styles. Lots of laughing – there was always a lot of laughing with Donald.

Syd Takayama (kneeling) next to Micky Ehrhardt and Skip Frye. In the back row, Cathi Webster, Donald, David Nuuheiwa, Jeannie Shanks with the trophy, Tom Webster. *Kevin Kinnear*

Donald loved his cars, especially this Corvette Stingray. *Kevin Kinnear*

I fondly remember a couple of the barbies we had at his Cleveland Street factory, which I'd visit whenever I was in Oceanside, Donald sloshing his famous 'Surfer's Choice Teriyaki' sauce on steaks while he told me about the latest board he'd shaped. His security dog, a Doberman named Winston, would run around barking, and Syd would yell at Donald to mind the flames and not burn the meat. It was always a cast of twenty or so – the talented workers who helped make Hawaiian Pro Designs, whatever surf stars were in town, the HPD team, even the odd homeless person. No one was turned away. Donald treated everyone he met with aloha and respect, unless they did wrong by him. He believed that we're all a part of a special brotherhood.

He called me at 4 a.m. just before he passed away in 2012, full of cheer like always, completely stoked. I hope Donald's vibe is infectious and filters down to new generations of surfers. I dearly miss him.

Whenever I've been in the States, I've gravitated to Malibu. It was the only place I felt comfortable in and more or less became my second home back in the winter of 1962–63, when Butch Linden's mother, Margaret, plucked me out of the clink, where I'd been put for being an illegal alien. Somehow, Immigration in Hawaii had allowed me to enter the US as a fifteen-year-old without a legal guardian. I stayed in the islands for three months that year, but when I arrived in Los Angeles I was arrested and put in jail until the problem could be sorted out. It seemed I needed a legal American mum, and Margaret Linden volunteered.

On that first trip, I didn't surf any of the three famous breaks at Surfrider Beach – First, Second or Third point. They're mainly summer breaks, when the swell is from the south. However, as the weeks stretched into a month, I got a taste of how incredible a wave at Malibu can be. It is the perfect point break – round river stones lining the bay, the waves breaking perpendicular from the shore for a couple of hundred metres. I was raised on beach breaks at Collaroy, on the Northern Beaches of Sydney, so getting to surf a point break like this was better than Christmas.

On another trip in the summer of 1967, the year after my World Championship win, I left my home in Oz looking for something. I wasn't quite sure exactly what, but it definitely called for a trip to the States. There was no such thing as a professional surfer back then; Midget was the only Australian who got paid to surf. In retrospect, I should have gone looking for a manager, but that didn't occur to me. I just knew in my heart that something good would happen if I hit the road. After all, I was the new world surfing champ.

Malibu was the logical place to start: it was the only place in America that I knew my way around. As well as the Linden family, I knew some members of the Malibu Surfing Association and Duke Boyd and Doris Moore from the Hang Ten surf clothing company. But that was it.

I'm not sure how it happened, but somehow Dewey Weber contacted me. It must have been through the Lindens. Margaret told me that Dewey wanted to buy me breakfast and have a talk about joining the Weber surf team. At the time the Weber team was strong, with more than 500 surfers from all over America riding for it. I had seen a tonne of red jackets with the distinctive Weber logo embroidered on the pocket.

As Margaret was talking about Dewey, I remembered that when I was around fourteen and my schoolmates and I were possessed by everything surf, I decided that having the Weber logo on my jacket was a big deal. A couple of my friends and I had actually copied it from an ad in the first issue of *Surfer* and silkscreened the logo onto old white T-shirts. We thought we were really cool.

The first time I met Dewey face-to-face was at a cafe in Santa Monica, not far from the pier. It was obviously a place he frequented often, usually after his early-morning go out at the Bu. He struck me as a fast-talking ball of energy, with his short blond hair combed straight back like an ageing gremmie. He was still wet from his morning constitutional.

Right off the bat, like a little dynamo, he shared his vision of what we were going to do together – how he made 100 boards a day and was gonna make me rich. Over liberal slurps of coffee to wash down a plate of bacon, eggs and hash browns, he proposed a deal: 200 bucks a week for two years. He would fly me back to the States from Oz once a year, or whenever he thought he needed me to visit surf shops. I could stay in a room at his house in Hermosa Beach. He would get his wife, Carol, or his foxy secretary, Meg, to type up a formal contract as soon as we got to his office.

It sounded good to me. I had nothing going on in America. I had no other options, and $200 was more than my Aussie sponsor paid me. Right then and there I agreed. It just felt right. Within an hour we were walking into his office next to the factory on Lincoln. I met the effervescent Carol and ogled Meg while she took notes from Dewey and me concerning the guts of the contract. I didn't sign right then, telling Dewey I would bring the contract with me to Hawaii in November. There were a few Weber boards shaped by Donald Takayama in the showroom rack. They looked special, in the way of all Donald's designs.

At that stage, I didn't really understand the whole concept of the Californian glide that a good longboard should deliver. It took me years to appreciate the subtleties of Donald's designs. Anyway, it didn't take long to sort out the contract between Dewey and me – ten minutes, from memory. Then he wheeled me out the back to meet the crew who made the boards. Harold Iggy was the man, the head shaper of a six-man stable. He was Hawaiian, cool, and drove a Porsche, just like one of Dewey's cars except newer. I wondered if Dewey would ever let me drive it. It never happened, even after I had an American licence.

The Webers had lots of cars. Dewey loved his Porsche. Carol drove a Chevy that she'd nicknamed 'the Plum Duck'. It was a bastard of a car that regularly broke down, coughing and spluttering, when we were driving back from ski trips at Mammoth.

The arrangement was that I could use the black company van when I was in America. I met the factory manager, Peter Dale, an Englishman and a very nice guy. There must have been fifty people working out back and twenty or thirty glassing racks. I was stunned when I walked through the factory that first day: the volume of work was amazing. I'd figured Dewey was kidding me when he said they did 100 boards a day. Now I understood he was telling the truth.

Dewey Weber and me, Malibu, 1968. *Leroy Grannis*

Dewey and his son Shea, 1972. *Weber family*

Dewey came from a humble background. He was raised in the South Bay, not far from his factory in Venice. In his youth he was the Duncan yo-yo champion three times over. He was also a champion wrestler, but surfing was his real forte. He started surfing the year I was born, 1947, and by the mid-50s was regarded as one of the best on the coast. His nickname was 'the Little Man on Wheels'. Dale Velzy was the hottest surfboard manufacturer in California then, and Dewey surfed his boards and lived in his factory.

Eventually, after Dale failed to stay on top of the rent and the Internal Revenue Service sold his gullwing Mercedes for back taxes, Dewey took over the factory. In 1960, he started Weber Surfboards. From the early to mid-'60s, the Weber Performer was one of the bestselling longboards in the world. It was the perfect longboard for the average surfer – flat, thin, wide and forgiving. Dewey made thousands of Performers, until the shortboard revolution brought the industry to its knees.

So that's how I met and got involved with the Little Man on Wheels. Our affair only lasted a few years, but he kept me laughing and treated me well. I did not get rich, but one summer I drove the black van with my new wife, Marilyn, and Mike Tabeling all the way from California to Florida, across the Gulf Coast and up the entire east coast.

The last time I saw Dewey was in the 1980s. I was over in the States for one of the early Oceanside longboard contests and he came up and grabbed me, then introduced me to his girlfriend. She was significantly taller than Dewey, with big boobs. When she gave us some space, I commented on them and he delivered a classic Dewey grin, from ear to ear. 'I thought you'd notice those,' he said.

8

SAN O

San Onofre, one of the birthplaces of our tribe on the US mainland, is located about halfway between Los Angeles and San Diego, right near the border of Orange County. In 1933, around when it was first surfed, it was still part of the Rancho Santa Margarita, a huge cattle ranch that encompassed almost 32 kilometres of coastline from Dana Point to Oceanside.

In 1952, the newly formed San Onofre Surfing Club fought a successful battle against the Marine Corps, which had leased the old ranch, and retained access to the beach. A few years down the track, in 1973, San O became a designated state park, which offered further protection. The downside was you had to pay for access to the beach; you still do.

From an Australian beachgoer's perspective, with our golden

sands and clear waters, it's hard to understand what all the fuss is about. It's a typical, desolate Mexican-ish looking beach with a rocky shoreline, bordered by a desert bluff of cactus and saltbush. Both the coastal train track and the Interstate-5 highway run within 100 metres of the beach, which means it's open to every tourist travelling between LA and San Diego.

But it's the history and the overall ambience of San O that make it such a memorable experience. As soon as you drop off the bitumen you're in 1933. Whenever I've visited, it has almost felt like I can sense the ghost of Dale Velzy lurking behind the bamboo. I imagine him sitting at one of the old picnic tables, hiding from the sun, having an in-depth rave with someone about the benefits of the twin fin he rode here in the early '50s.

The two or three palm-frond shacks that dot the beach have looked that way forever – the same as when Marge Calhoun was being chased by Hevs McClennan, or when 'Burrhead' was taking a swig of moonshine straight from the bottle, sitting on the fender of a '38 Auburn Speedster. Folks would come and stay for weeks at a stretch, playing Hawaiian guitars, dancing, and drinking no small amount of alcohol. Have a look at a pictures of Mary Hawkins gliding into deep water out the back at Old Man's, or the shot of the San O crew setting the world record for the most people on a wave. This is where Dora learnt to surf, for goodness sake. The beach has a proud history.

It's a miracle that a place like San O still exists in Southern California in 2018. Developers have been trying to put a toll road through the park for decades, and surfers and greenies have successfully stopped that for the time being. But with the population explosion in Southern California, I suppose the road is inevitable.

San Onofre, the birthplace of surfing in Southern California, 2018. *Tara Torburn*

For now, though, it still looks exactly like it did when I first visited in 1966, which fills me with some degree of confidence. Perhaps surfing has gained a little more credence in America. Either that, or we're just growing in numbers – at least to the degree that we can't be pushed around or ignored by the authorities. Certainly,

the attitude of the California State Parks reflects this change in
attitude. With some luck and good management, perhaps this
unique beach will be preserved for the second, third and fourth
generations of the surfing families who frequent San Onofre every
chance they get.

Everyone who surfs here regularly cares about the beach a lot.

It's their lifeblood. They virtually live there in the summer. As a San O local told me once, 'They're never gonna let anyone pave the parking lot. It's dirt. You gotta drive slow. Don't raise no dust. Take it all in. Relax and enjoy the sights.'

When you see a mate's car, or someone you wouldn't mind having a chat with, you find a spot among the other devotees and cruise. Most people back their cars in towards the beach – it's the best way to check the surf, especially if you have a van or an RV or a pick-up truck with a tailgate. You ask someone – anyone, really – about how it's looking out there and they generally take the time to tell you. It seems that the surfing fraternity at San Onofre has loads of time. They have their priorities straight, clearly.

The waves break over a series of reefs, with a bastard of a shore break. It's not the worst, mind you. It's just really annoying, even when the surf is only 3 feet (1 metre). Everyone gets bitten on the ankles trying to navigate the small, football-shaped stones at the shoreline. It seems you gotta get a bit of bark off to have the complete San O experience.

Barney Wilkes playing guitar with the San O crew. *California Surf Museum collection*

San O in September 1949, always a great spot to hang out. From left to right, Lloyd Murray,
Bob 'Ole' Olson and Don Mincey. *California Surf Museum collection*

The reefs change a lot with the tides and the swell. Just north, there are also the perfect set-ups at Trestles – Uppers, Lowers and Church. Running south from the fence that divides the military from the commoners, you have Sandbar Mecca, the Point, Four Doors, Old Man's, Dogpatch, Nukes and Trails, in that order. The actual wave types to the south are all very similar: submerged reef with a shifting sand coating. Because it changes so much, some days at one break are better than others.

The second to last of these breaks is called Nukes because it sits right in front of the decommissioned Edison nuclear plant. The reactors are shaped like 60-metre-tall breasts and so the plant is nicknamed 'Dolly Parton'. They really do look like a set of perfect, gigantic tits, complete with nipples, and in my wildest nightmares they have the ability to wipe out everyone in the closest city, San Clemente. Perhaps there's a lesson here for innocent little boys: be careful of big boobs and their powers.

Dolly came online in 1968 but no one seems to know if she's now leaking radiation. One thing is for sure: the reactors are cooled by saltwater, which is taken into the plant and then discharged back into the ocean. The process makes the water at Nukes warm, even in the dead of winter. There have been loads of shark sightings in the area and a few attacks, but surfers still ride waves at all the breaks every day. Apparently at the wrong time of year hundreds of baby lobsters can be seen washed up on the beach, red and cooked. I hope it's the hot water that kills them and not radiation.

Despite all this, San O is still one of the few places in the world where aloha is alive and well. It's always a pleasure to come back every year and see this part of surfing's heritage thriving, especially when the sun goes down on a weekend in summer. The San Onofre Surfing Club has somewhere between 800 and 900 members, depending on the season. It was officially formed in 1952 by Andre 'Frenchy' Jahan and the legendary Barney Wilkes, but hundreds of like-minded families have been gathering at the beach since the 1920s.

All the serious members have the club's tattoo on their right arm. They are vocal about the direction of their beach. Everyone I have spoken with takes it seriously, but that commitment aside, the club has a pretty heavy social calendar. They're also civic-minded. As well as maintaining the institution of the grass shacks, the club has preserved the 'fire pits' that are spread out at intervals along the beach and play an important part in the ritual, especially in winter. You have to bring your own wood these days, and you can't stay overnight any more.

I was sitting around one of these fires in the 1960s when I first heard Terry 'Tubesteak' Tracy tell the story of Gidget. The real version is a classic.

Kathy Kohner was born in Los Angeles in 1941. Her parents were Czechoslovakian Jews who had fled the Holocaust. Her dad, Frederick, had a PhD in psychology, and in California he got a job writing screenplays and lecturing at the University of California. His daughter was his pride and joy, and as soon as she was old enough, she was given a car and a new baby-blue Hobie surfboard.

In the summer of 1956, when she was about fifteen, Kathy constantly hung around the wall at Malibu alongside some of the best surfers in the world. There wasn't much of her to look at, so she was teased pretty heavily when she first came to the beach. She was only 5 feet (152 centimetres) tall and maybe 95 pounds (43 kilograms). Tubesteak nicknamed her Gidget – a girl midget.

She spent all of that summer driving to the store to buy ingredients to make sandwiches for the crew. She was persistent, though, and learnt how to stand up and angle on a wave after just a few weeks. Gidget had been bitten by the surf bug. Pretty soon she became proficient.

At home, she raved to her dad about the surf scene at Malibu. He was fascinated with the story and decided to write about his daughter's adventures. By 1957, Frederick had the story of Kathy's escapades at Malibu composed into a novel, and it sold half a million copies. Everyone loved it – another generation had discovered surfing.

After the first *Gidget* movie came out in 1959, surfing was happening all over America and the prestigious magazine *Life* did a story on Kathy. The success of the first couple of *Gidget* films convinced all the other studios in Hollywood to get into the game too, and it wasn't long before it became difficult to get any time to shoot on the beach at Malibu.

Frankie Avalon and Annette Funicello made a series of 'beach party' movies that became iconic. As I mentioned earlier, Miki Dora was employed to do the surfing as a double for Frankie. At one point, as he was shooting a scene, Miki kept telling the camera boat to come closer and closer to get a tighter shot of the surf action. Of course the inevitable happened: the boat capsized in the shore break, spilling the director, the cameraman and all the 35-millimetre camera equipment into the surf.

Miki had set the whole thing up. He came back that night under a full moon and retrieved the equipment, washed it out and used a third party to sell it back to the insurance company. He also capitalised on Annette's little insecurities. Apparently she had to have $1000 in her trailer at all times. When Dora found out about this, he came up through the trapdoor under the trailer and pinched the money. He was never caught for this little scam.

Stealing to support your surfing habit goes back to our roots. Way back before the auto makers made it prohibitive by modifying their fuel tanks, my mates and I often siphoned petrol from any car we could. In my youth, I also recall taking milk money from outside people's houses while they slept. These crimes were committed just to get to the surf.

In Hawaii, Captain Cook had problems with the natives stealing from his ship. He was forty-eight years old when he went ashore to retrieve a small boat that the Hawaiians had absconded with. The Hawaiians clubbed him to death. They have always been warlike, and they are a strong root in surfing's family tree.

I sincerely hope that San Onofre can survive the onslaught of the developers in Southern California. In this day and age, I am sure it will be difficult, but I am an optimist. Surely it's a matter of balance. I choose to think that the authorities will see the necessity to protect San O just as the owners of The Ranch, north of Santa Barbara, have done. Controlling the number of visitors to a sensitive environment is very important.

9

RUSSELL HUGHES
AND DAPPA

The first time I met Russell Hughes, I found myself riding with him on the back of a flatbed truck from Bulahdelah to Sydney with my good friend John Witzig. It was probably 1963 – could have been '64. Exactly how Russ ended up with us on the tail end of our surf trip to Queensland escapes me.

John and I were on a surfari to Noosa Heads, and I guess Russ had organised with John to get a lift to Sydney. Two-thirds of the way to the city, we blew up Mrs Witzig's VW beetle, which John borrowed regularly to go on our surfaris. After a day of dicking around in Bulahdelah, we were forced to leave the thing behind.

For some reason, a nice truckie took pity on us. That's how the three of us ended up on the back of the flatbed, hiding under a tarpaulin to protect us from the driving rain, huddled close to the cab, bouncing up and down on the old two-lane Pacific Highway. In those days, it was a good four hours to Sydney. All those pies and Cokes from the previous days had created a gastric problem for Russ and me, and the situation was driving John mad. We were both farting like troopers.

At first it was funny and Russ and I were laughing hysterically. However, every time one of us would let one go under the tarp, John would explode, pulling back the cover, gasping for air and punching the arm of the person he thought was responsible. Usually, John was not sure exactly who had dropped the fart. I suppose it was whichever one of us looked the guiltiest. The accused would scream with indignation at the suggestion that he was responsible for the pungent smell: 'It wasn't me! It was him!'

So it went on under the tarp for hours. Good fun, but in retrospect I think you had to be there to appreciate this level of humour. Russell said he had been raised in a circus. He knew some really dirty jokes and all the words to a couple of songs, one of which I have never forgotten: '26 Miles (Santa Catalina)'.

After that trip, Russ and I became pretty tight mates. We didn't do much surfing together while he was staying in Sydney. I lived in Collaroy and he was staying on the Peninsula, so we were 16 kilometres apart.

Russ landed a job sanding boards for one of the surfboard makers in Brookvale. A few months later, he moved back up to his home state of Queensland and was sanding boards for Hayden Kenny at Caloundra. I went back and forth between Sydney and the Sunshine Coast pretty regularly, so we hung out and surfed.

Russ wasn't much of a competitor. He did okay, but he wasn't ruthless enough – he was more of a soul surfer. He did win an early Mattara contest, though. The best thing about that event was seeing Russ step out of a car on the main beach of Newcastle, dressed exactly like the Beatles on the album cover of *Sgt. Pepper's Lonely Hearts Club Band.*

Other than that win, the best contest result he had in Australia was a third in the 1966 Australian National Titles, which were held on a good right-hand sandbank in the middle of Coolangatta Beach on the Gold Coast. That result meant he qualified for the Australian team for the 1968 World Championship in Puerto Rico.

Russell had no way of getting there, but luckily he met an entrepreneur who offered to pay his air ticket. Gareth Powell was not a surfer: he was a young, wealthy English gentleman with a desire to get into the publishing business in Australia. To this end, as I have mentioned, he employed John Witzig to create and edit *Surf International* for him. At the time I knew nothing about this generous offer from Gareth. It must have been extended after I left Australia on the *Evolution* trip with John's brother Paul.

When Russell turned up in Puerto Rico with his then girlfriend, Trisha Thompson, I was surprised and totally stoked. They had travelled from Australia to California, where they spent a month in North County, San Diego. Russell had a beautiful Bob McTavish surfboard with him. It was 8 feet (2.4 metres) long and a little narrow for my liking, but I did not doubt that he would make it work.

He was surfing well everywhere he went in PR. Mostly, he looked like a cat that had just been dropped onto something solid – crouching low, running free on the big smooth faces. Photographic evidence of how well Russell surfed in Puerto Rico is readily available.

ABC's Wide World of Sports was the number one TV sports show in the States at the time. The nationally televised program was pretty accurate in its coverage of how the contest came down, showing a contrast in longboards and shortboards and the two different styles, traditional versus radical.

In the final, Russell's surfing was smooth and stylish and he managed to stroke into some of the bigger waves. From my perspective out in the water, I thought he could have won under the judging system we had at that time, but when the results were announced, he came in third – a placing he seemed quite happy with.

Russell and Trisha took the long way home and eventually arrived back in Byron Bay. Marilyn and I moved to Byron in 1969 when Russ was already living there, shacked up with Garth Murphy and Nyarie Abbey in a magnificent old house behind Newrybar. It was a perfect example of a typical, high-quality Australian farmhouse – beautiful hardwood floors, and giant rooms with picture rails and 3.6-metre ceilings. As was the fashion in that era, the interior rooms were closed off to the sun but a big, wide veranda ran all the way around the house. It was a wonderful place to sit and let the world go by. The garden was full of 100-year-old cycads and all manner of other rainforest plants that flourished in the dappled sunlight.

The relationship between Nyarie, Garth and Russell when they were living together was very harmonious, but after a few months Russell moved closer to the beach with Trisha. They were on a small farm just past the honey man, a kilometre further towards Lennox Head from the Broken Head turn-off.

Marilyn and I had been talking about leaving Sydney for years, even before we were married. Every time I had a few days off, we

Russell Hughes aka Tony Wayne Scheling. *Nyarie Abbey*

Standing: Trisha Thompson and Russ. Sitting: Robert Conneeley, Nyarie Abbey, John Witzig. *Paul Carey*

went to Byron, enjoying the area and looking at real estate. By '69 we were spending more time there than in Sydney. Eventually we found an old farmhouse on the first ridge out of town, overlooking the ocean.

We finally plucked up the courage to cut ties with the Northern Beaches, renting out our beautiful home in Whale Beach and moving to Byron Bay permanently. It was a big deal. I had managed to talk Marilyn into throwing in her schoolteaching job, and together with my young brother Chris, we packed up our new kombi, which we had sent home from Europe, and left Sydney for good.

Marilyn and I had honeymooned in Europe, driving the kombi all over. It was a comfortable vehicle with all the bells and whistles, making it perfect for a few days camping. The only time we had anything weird happen was when we were camped in a pine forest behind La Barre in France. Some friends picked me up early to go surfing before dawn, and I left Marilyn asleep in the kombi. When we returned several hours later, she was totally freaked out. Some guy with a gun had come to the window and she awoke to see him staring at her. She screamed and he eventually left, but it was obviously a traumatic experience.

They were wild times in Byron in the early '70s. Russ, Bill Engler, Garth and I used to claim that we were just like Native American braves. I won't explain who Bill and Garth are as I wrote about both of them extensively in my autobiography, *Nat's Nat* – suffice to say they were committed surfers who had roomed together in college in Santa Barbara and came to live in Byron in 1969. Unlike many young Americans, they actually made their dreams happen.

We lived in a sort of Native American camp. We each had our own houses with our own space. When the surf looked promising,

we went on raiding parties, chasing waves together. Our individual homes were spread along an 800-metre stretch of exposed
ridge overlooking Broken Head. When the conditions looked right
from my end of the ridge, I would let the rest of the tribe know.
Sometimes I would ride my horse down to the beach and along to
Broken Head. It was easy to tether my steed, retrieve my board
from under the tree where I'd left it the day before, and paddle
out. It was an idyllic lifestyle, for sure.

Normally we would set out early in the morning and drive the
whole coast to find the best waves possible. After tracking them
down, we'd spend the rest of the day riding them. This took many
hours and a knowledge of the conditions, balancing the wind,
tide and swell, working with the limitations of the boards we had.
Sometimes the quest would take us as far south as Ballina's south
wall. The paddle across the Richmond River was a freak-out
because of the possibility of sharks. But it was quicker than the
alternative – a tiny, four-car punt across the river.

There were perhaps another twenty surfers living in the Byron
area at that time. We all knew each other and hung out on social
occasions, but when it came to actually surfing, a lot of times you
did it on your own or with just one mate. Sometimes we felt like
we were the only surfers on the planet.

You have to remember this was pre leg-ropes and pre fin
boxes and we were surfing directly in front of exposed rocks,
which was not for the faint-hearted. Lennox Head (Lenny) was a
serious adrenaline jolt. At 10 feet (3 metres), it was an unforgiving
beast. One error in judgement meant a swim for sure, and more
than likely a couple of dings and even the loss of the fin. I used to
carry resin and roving fibreglass in my car – all the equipment to
put a fin back on. One time I sanded the detached fin on a rock,

smoothed it out with a Surform blade and was back in the line-up, all within twenty minutes. That was my personal best.

There are still loads of protected little beaches in the area between Ballina and Brunswick Heads. In the '70s, we would push through the bush and come out on a bald bluff with fair little rights or left-handers. The quality of these beaches all depended on the shape of the sandbanks. Constant north-easters in the summer built up the sand against the points, and then the dominant southerlies of winter sculpted the banks into perfect triangles.

Besides Lenny, the only other point break we surfed consistently was the Pass. It was nicknamed 'the Horse's Arse'. Mostly it was a social beach, where you saw all your mates and hung out with girls. It was very user-friendly. Sometimes scores of punters would be clambering all over the rocks, searching for the best perch to watch the performances. The rocks themselves rarely claimed a board: even though the take-off was close to some extremely sharp volcanic rocks, the wave ran away very quickly into the wide-open bay of Byron. Many times, I took off right on the rocks and never actually hit them. After that, the ride was over sand for the next couple of hundred metres. Sharp, rocky take-offs with sand points like the Pass are what make northern New South Wales and southern Queensland unique in Australia. This situation does not exist consistently anywhere else in the country, at least not that I am aware of.

The river mouth at Brunswick Heads is some twenty minutes up the coast. That was as far north as we ventured. It was really pushing the envelope. On huge swells we'd go to the Goldy, but only a few times a year. Even in those days, the crowds put us right off. When the wind was from the west, the Pass had a heavy chop on the face. This was the norm for early mornings – we called it 'morning sickness'. Most times, by 10 a.m. the wind had gone more south, which made the surface conditions straight offshore.

By 1990, Russell was sick. He had been diagnosed with bowel cancer while he was living in Mexico and it forced him to move back to California so he could receive the finest treatment possible at Scripps, in San Diego. After the treatment he relocated again, back to Australia, first settling in Margaret River and then moving back to Byron in 1994.

One day he called me at Angourie and said he would like me to drive up and spend a day with him. We surfed Broken Head. He was still surfing smoothly and accurately. We sat in the morning sun, looking out at twenty people in a surf school and another ten labouring in the marginal conditions. We talked about the old days when we had often surfed Broken all on our own with high-quality waves. He showed me his colostomy bag and told me he now knew how Bob Evans had felt all those years before.

Russ had been with the same French-Canadian woman, Monique Roy, for years. She had come to Byron in the early '70s from Montreal and turned out to be extremely loyal to Russ. With the cancer not improving, they moved back to Canada to be close to her family, who were very supportive. We only spoke one more time before he died. He sounded upbeat and had resigned himself to the fact that he had enjoyed a good life and it was going to end soon.

Russ died in May 2011. His only child, Kokee, had flown to Canada to spend the last year of Russell's life hanging out with his dad. When he died, Kokee called me to pass on the sad news. The dreaded cancer had struck again. Society really needs a cure for this devastating disease.

Kokee is still living in Byron, on the same ridge that his dad shared with Garth, Bill and me. Being a child of the '70s, he is totally absorbed in all the pleasures of that amazing town, which is still not so different from what we had back then. There's just a million times more people to share it with now. I don't mean that in a derogatory sense.

Russ and I had one adventure that will stick in my mind forever. A few months after Marilyn and I moved to Byron, he and I packed up the kombi to drive to the 1970 Bells Beach contest. We were totally ready for another good adventure. We'd had a good look at a map to find the most remote place on the south coast of New South Wales or Victoria. It turned out to be Wilsons Promontory.

At that time, Russell and I would have to be described as a couple of tripped-out hippies. Somehow, somewhere along the way, we managed to acquire a cheeky young grommet named Grant 'Dappa' Oliver. We had stopped at Narrabeen for a quick surf on the way down the coast and I ended up having a chat to Dappa in the car park. I didn't know him at all at that point, other than that he was a good little surfer from Narrabeen who had the potential to be much better.

When he asked me for a lift to Bells, I had some reservations but ultimately said yes, thinking back to the times when older surfers had helped me out. Dappa was many years younger than Russ and me. He was short and stocky, a little powerhouse, especially when he took off deep and opened up, turning down the line.

He said he was desperate. All his mates had already left for Bells and he really needed a lift. I made it clear that Russell and I were keen to spend a few days in the isolation of Wilsons Promontory, a plan that included ingesting some strong psychedelic mushrooms that we had preserved in honey. We had a healthy stash of food and were totally prepared for a few days camping out.

Loaded with boards and sleeping bags, the three of us set out on foot from the end of the road. There were only a few shacks, and they were more than a kilometre and a half from the coast. I remember how rugged the landscape was – dense bush, with huge granite boulders lunging out of the ocean. Maybe the mushrooms we'd gobbled made it all more intense.

About halfway down the track, we found a beach that was completely deserted. The surf was nothing special, with lots of rips pulling the waves in every possible direction. Close-out sets crashed between the boulders. We surfed when we could. Dappa was ripping. He was in training for the Bells contest but Russell and I were as high as kites, most of the time rolling around and laughing at nothing in particular.

For the next couple of days, we went completely back to nature. We surfed naked and slept on the beach with a big fire. The place was incredibly beautiful but the isolation started to drive Dappa crazy. He told us more than once that we were fucking idiots, and kept asking when we were getting back on the road – he didn't want to miss his heat at Bells. Eventually a southerly buster came through and we ran for the van.

Because he didn't partake of any drugs on our camping trip, Dappa had a totally different perspective. Russell and I laughed at him, and considered him a full-on, cheeky grommet. One thing was for sure: by the time we drove into the Bells car park, young Dappa was over hanging out with a couple of old hippies. He vaulted out of the side door of the kombi, stoked to get back to his mates from Narrabeen. Later, he came back to pick up his gear and surfboard. That was the last I ever saw of him. He finished up doing pretty well at Bells, coming in third behind Andrew McKinnon and Michael Peterson; Michael won the juniors at Bells that year.

A couple of years later I heard that Dappa had made the team for the 1972 World Championship in San Diego. He finished second in the Australian Junior Titles in order to achieve that honour. That same year, on the way home from California, I heard he stopped in Hawaii and placed third in the prestigious Smirnoff contest in big Haleiwa – a great result for young Dap. No one in Hawaii would have ever heard of him prior to that.

Grant 'Dappa' Oliver. *John Witzig*

In the mid-1980s Dappa married his girlfriend, Debbie, and had two kids, Allison and Matthew. He was trying to live a normal life. They were set up in Narrabeen, but he was surfing less and less. Dappa was always smart academically. He was one of the brightest students at Narrabeen Boys High School, but he suffered with depression.

Over the years he had proven that he was an exceptional footballer, and he took on the big boys playing Rugby League for the Narrabeen Sharks. Word was that he was a hell of a halfback. At some point, he gave up surfing altogether and moved to Corowa on the Murray River, a long way from the ocean. He started teaching school and continued playing football for the local Rugby League team. Apparently he was a popular bloke, but his marriage had fallen apart.

Dappa ended up an alcoholic and took his own life in 1994. There was not much talk of his suicide in the surfing world, other than among his mates at Narrabeen. Certainly he deserves recognition for what he achieved as a surfer. I know that a lot of older surfers, and his family, would feel much better if Surfing Australia recognised Dappa's contribution.

10

BELLS

The first time I went to Bells was Easter of 1963, the second year
of the event. John Witzig and I somehow scammed our way into
the back seat of a little Simca sedan owned by a guy named Tojo.
Tojo intended to make a movie and he wanted some film of me
surfing. If he did shoot something, I never saw it.

Neither John nor I had met Tojo before the trip. All we knew
was that he was from Bronte, on the south side of Sydney. He and his
shotgun mate were good blokes. Fellow surfers, they helped us out
by giving us a lift all the way from Sydney to Bells. In those days, it
seemed that just about every surfer in Oz made the pilgrimage to Bells
for Easter. It was just what you did: the annual gathering of the tribe.

There were only a few thousand of us in that tribe in Australia
at the time and we were outcasts. The clubbies hated us because

we were rebels. So many surfers had left the lifesaving clubs all over Australia that the clubs thought the numbers of surfers had become a problem for them. With the decline in membership and dues they felt vulnerable, but there was nothing they could do about it. I suppose their worry was that without a constant flow of young blood, they could lose the ownership of their beachfront properties. To this day, the surf lifesaving clubs stand on the most prestigious real estate in Australia.

Back then, in the cities, the surfers hated the clubbies because the clubbies confiscated boards whenever someone surfed between the flags. Even when no one was swimming in that area, they still took our boards for a week. The long and short of it was that not all surfers wanted to be a part of the structure and regimentation of the surf clubs. Learning basic lifesaving skills was another matter, and most surfers saw the necessity of that training. I felt, and still feel, it should be taught in schools.

If you were a young man in the '60s with the opportunity to spend considerable time at the beach, choosing between the regimentation of the surf clubs and the freedom of riding a board was easy. In the early part of the decade, the mainstream media did not have a clue about surfing or surfers – they just made up stories to sell newspapers. For example, the battle between the rockers and the surfies was all media hype. Consequently, surfers closed ranks. We banded together, just like the bikies today. We knew we were different and in the minority. We were a brotherhood. If anyone was stuck on the side of the road with surfboards on their roof, you stopped to help them out. They were members of the same tribe and you gave them a hand.

For the most part, the drive down to Victoria with Tojo was uneventful: mile after mile in a cramped little car, bumping along the old two-lane highway between Sydney and Melbourne. At

nearly every servo when we stopped for petrol we saw other
surfers. We'd honk our horn as they screamed past, and they'd
do the same to us. It seemed like there were hundreds of us on the
road to Bells from Sydney.

The infamous Torquay camping ground in the early '60s. *Young family*

Glynn Ritchie (centre) leaving the water after winning the junior division at the
1963 Bells contest. *Young family*

After fifteen hours, we were relieved when we pulled into the Torquay camping ground. It was where everyone stayed before the advent of professional surfing, and was a vibrant part of the Bells contests in the '60s – the social hub for all the contestants before the pub kicked off. Nestled behind the sand dunes under low trees, the campsites and cabins were protected from the biting winds.

I think the main reason the camping area was so popular with holidaymakers and contestants was its closeness to the pub. It was just across the street from Torquay's only watering hole, Pawson's Torquay Hotel, which meant you could get pissed and stumble home or, if you got lucky and managed to pull a chick, it wasn't too far to go to your campsite.

The pub was a home away from home for all the interstate surfers. Every afternoon following the contest, we would go have a couple of schooners of Victoria Bitter to celebrate a win or drown our sorrows. After the afternoon piss-up, all the crew who were still standing hit the shower block to get cleaned up and catch a perv on the available chicks.

We arrived right on dusk that first night. The pub wasn't going off yet so we headed straight for the glow of a huge bonfire that was blazing in the centre of a sea of tents. It was a who's who of Australian surfing. I knew some of them – Bobby Brown, Garry Birdsall from Cronulla, and a couple of dozen other blokes from the south side, including Muscles, Natch, Bobcat and Ugg from the Maroubra area. Joe Larkin, Furry, PT, Keith Paull, the Neilsen brothers, Tony Dempsey, Peter Drouyn and a young Michael Peterson made up a hot-shot crew from the Gold Coast. It was good fun – so many faces in the light of the fire, some of them sitting on stumps of wood or on the bonnet of their car, others hanging out in their sleeping bags.

I noticed a couple of guys from the north side of Sydney who I knew vaguely. I had seen their faces out in the surf at Narrabeen. Manly's Nipper Williams and Mexican Sumpter – who was the older brother of Rodney 'Gopher' Sumpter, one of my best friends from school – were verbally sparring with each other, which was very entertaining for the crowd. While Mex was distracted with one of his over-the-top raves, Nipper slid around behind him and poked the end of Mex's sleeping bag onto the coals of the fire. Next minute Mex jumped up, his sleeping bag smouldering. You had to be on your guard with all the pranksters around the camping ground at Easter.

All the frivolity was gone the next morning. The fire was charred to embers and bleary-eyed girls and boys were climbing out of cars, groping for their clothing. Everyone was looking for a cuppa before heading down to Bells.

Thinking back on that first morning's drive around the cliffs from Torquay to Bells, I don't believe I had seen a solid ground-swell before. Growing up on the Northern Beaches of Sydney, you would have thought real swell was something that occurred every now and then, but I honestly can't remember anything that resembled those long lines stretching for mile after mile, stacked up all the way to the horizon. Both John and I were stunned by the beauty and the power. It was a sight to behold.

Bells is shaped like a giant amphitheatre, making it the best place to watch a surf contest that I have ever seen. There are so many places to clamber up the sandy cliffs for a perfect vantage point. I can't remember the quality of the waves for the contest in 1963 but I think it was still pretty good by the time they were running heats. Nothing will ever compare with that first sight of an 8-foot (2.4-metre) groundswell pouring into Bells ahead of the event.

The first Bells was held in 1962, making it now the longest-running surf contest in Australia, possibly the world. Glynn Ritchie won the men's division that first year; he also won the juniors. He was the only surfer I knew who made the drive to Bells from Sydney in 1962. A couple of Manly Bower boys, Ken Bate and Robbie Lane, went along for the ride.

The following year, I finished second behind Glynn in the juniors. He had grown up living with his mother and his aunt in a spacious apartment overlooking Fairy Bower on Sydney's Northern Beaches. It was the perfect environment for him to become a committed surfer. During the time we worked together

shaping boards at Gordon Woods we became close mates. Every weekend we would leave Sydney and drive to the south coast of New South Wales.

Those trips were full of excitement – riding every wave we came across, no matter how big or small, jumping back in Glynn's car, him doing four-wheel drifts on all the dirt roads he could find. He could burn rubber shifting into second gear, and loved to drive fast, fanging down the old Princes Highway in his hotted-up Cortina sedan before there was a speed limit. He was a great driver and it was one of his passions. Glynn was always proud of his cars. I remember the day he pulled up at work in his dream ride – a brand-new 179 Holden station wagon. He took me for a spin and I was impressed.

Perfect corduroy all the way to the horizon, the old stagecoach track running along the top of the cliffs from Torquay to Bells, alongside the new sealed road it is today. *Steve Ryan*

Glynn Ritchie and Maria. *Ritchie family*

In the early 1980s, Glynn fell in love with Papua New Guinea. Together with his wife, Shirley, and their daughter, Gemma, he sailed his 35-foot (10-metre) yacht to PNG and never really came back. His second daughter, Jessica, was born in PNG but the marriage fell apart. He had a thriving business with fibreglass fabrication and formed a close bond with a local girl named Maria, who was from Mount Hagen in the highlands. Unfortunately, Glynn started smoking cigarettes in his fifties and died of emphysema in Sydney in June 2017.

One of my early heroes, Doug Andrew, won the men's division at Bells in 1963. He was a big, solid, football-type guy. Doug and his brother Jeff hailed from Dee Why. Doug was a fearless charger in the big surf at Dee Why Point. The Andrew family was a strong surf-club family, but it seemed to me they loved to ride waves more than being clubbies.

Mick Dooley was the next Bells champ, in 1964. His cool, no-nonsense style of surfing was so worthy of the win. I watched on in appreciation from the juniors division. I think '64 was also the year some guy dressed up as Superman and surfed right through the competition area. We all loved it. I was out in the water in a semifinal and the guy on the microphone was screaming at a surfer sitting way out the back off Centreside, telling him to paddle in and stay out of the competition area. All of a sudden a huge set loomed on the horizon and I saw this guy in a cape take off and come streaking down the line. I think they gave him the £1 prize for the best wave of the contest.

Bondi's Robert Conneeley was the same age as me. His nickname was Bonza and he was a good mate. His dad, Reg, was a classic. In the early '60s, they invited me to their holiday shack down past Sussex Inlet on the south coast of New South Wales. We had a great time surfing a little right-hand reef break that is probably still called Conneeley's. Reg taught me how to catch fish, clean and cook them. I was impressed, as my own dad never did anything like that with me.

When we were in the water, Bonz and I competed against each other. It was serious fun seeing who could get the best wave. He always had a style of his own, precise and artistic. In '64 he beat me, winning the juniors at the World Championship in Sydney, and did it again in '65 in the open men's at Bells. That was the big year. They cancelled the juniors due to the size of the waves. I remember Glynn Ritchie, Bonz and I trying to get out through the shore break, with big, solid masses of whitewater pounding us. The waves were relentless but I finally got a break and slid out. I was terrified. The horizon was black and I spent the next ten minutes scratching over giant feathering lips. I was so glad when

I turned my head and saw Bonza paddling up a wave face on his knees behind me. We were both in the thick of it – a potentially life-threatening situation, stuck out the back until we could safely paddle inside and take off on a little one.

A few years later Bonz gave up competition, sold his surf shop in Bondi, packed up his house on the back of a Toyota truck and, together with his beautiful wife, Di, spent years on the road all over Australia. They raised two lovely daughters along the way and eventually settled in the Margaret River area of Western Australia. I always thought Bonza was the perfect role model for a surfer. He lived totally by his convictions and was the true essence of what being a surfer is, no matter his age.

I won Bells for the next couple of years. I know what a fight it was because my mate Ted Spencer (who won in 1968 and 1969) and I often talked fondly of our battles to get the best waves. I got the better of Ted in 1970. In 1971 the Gold Coast's maestro, Paul 'Smelly' Neilsen, tumbled out of a limo a few minutes before the final. He had come straight from a disco in Melbourne, and was still half pissed but he surfed like a man possessed and put on a great show. Some people were amazed he won in that condition, but not me. I knew what a party animal Smelly was. Terry Fitzgerald blitzed them in 1972, the Sultan of Speed running flat out from Rincon to the Bowl. Then it was MP's turn, three years in a row – 1973, 1974 and 1975. He blew us all away with his extraordinary talent.

To be honest, I lost interest when Bells went professional in 1973. The innocence I had enjoyed on our annual pilgrimages turned into something I could no longer relate to. Right from the first Bells contest, the judging was subjective. Most of the competitors could do the same moves but it was their individual styles that set them apart. Everyone had such a unique approach in those days. It really depended on whose style was in vogue as to whether you won or not. However, after the contest became professional, the judging changed: then it was assessed on the number of manoeuvres a surfer did on the wave.

The majority of surfers who won Bells in the '60s and '70s had shaped their own surfboards. We all thought long and hard about the conditions at Bells, then designed and shaped our boards to show our best surfing. I don't think this has generally happened in other sporting competitions, past or present. I certainly can't think of one. No one else uses handmade equipment. Perhaps that is why we saw such dramatic changes in the equipment being ridden by everyday surfers during this period. We were constantly experimenting, feeding off each other, trying something new whenever possible. Hanging out together at the annual Bells contest was really important to advancing the design of our equipment, sometimes even swapping boards for a few waves. This interaction between most of the quality surfers was critical to advancing Australian surfing.

Funny, the things I remember from the old days at Bells. Naturally I remember the girls. Then there was the scratching for the horizon on the big days. And also the year the contest was moved to Fishos (Fishermans Beach) because it was too big and stormy at Bells itself. You wouldn't believe it if you took a look at Fishos under normal conditions – it's a boat harbour, for goodness sake. But let me assure you, it does get good waves on rare occasions.

One thing's for sure: everyone who won a prized Bells trophy surfed their guts out to do it. There was no easy ride. From 2 to 15 feet (0.6 to 4.5 metres), the contest has always been a battle, moving all over the coast from Johanna to Fishos to find the most challenging waves. Bells is much more than just another contest – it's an institution. That kudos comes with age, miles on the clock, and being consistent. Like some wines, you don't just get there with one vintage. You can't reach that level with just one contest. It's like stripes in the army: you have to earn them.

Rip Curl took over the contest in the early 1970s. The original owners of the company, Doug 'Claw' Warbrick and Brian 'Sing Ding' Singer, kept the event running even when they didn't have the money in the bank to clear the cheques they gave out. They have both always been surfers through and through, and it shows in the attitude of their company. I remember when they told Michael Peterson and me that we could get free Rip Curl product forever, regardless of other sponsorships we might have in the future. I could get a new wetsuit anytime. You'll always be warm in the water, they told me. And that went for my family, too. I was stoked and ended up getting lots of wetsuits for my kids as they changed shape growing up.

Michael, on the other hand, didn't have kids. He was just very dedicated to his mum, Joan. After beating his heroin addiction, Michael was not in good shape. He was in and out of rehab, still living with Joan in Tweed Heads in humble conditions. Never being one to look a gift horse in the mouth, however, Michael decided that he would ask Rip Curl to send him a few different wetsuits in many different sizes every month. Michael and his mum sold them at the monthly Gold Coast markets, and the money helped Joan out with living expenses. This worked like a charm for six months. I think Michael thought Rip Curl didn't notice or didn't care about the number of suits he was getting.

When I heard about the scam, I thought that Sing Ding and Claw would feel they had been taken advantage of and stop the flow of rubber. But no. Like I said, they were both surfers. They understood Michael's situation and decided they could afford a few wetsuits every month to help him get through a particularly rough patch.

In the same vein, the company has supported the Bells contest for as long as it's been going. It's in their DNA, and I'm sure they will be doing it for as long as pro surfing exists.

11

PUERTO RICO, FRANCE, TAHITI

The 1968 World Surfing Championship in Puerto Rico was significant because it was the first international exhibition after the so-called shortboard revolution. As I've said before, this is actually a terrible misnomer, and the real story was about much more than the size of the board.

While it is true that the average length of a surfboard had shrunk by about 3 feet (1 metre) by 1970, the true developments came from various improvements in the design of boards, allowing for a radical shift in the way a wave could be ridden. But the media needed a label, and 'shortboard revolution' was the phrase they grasped to describe the dramatic changes that were on display in Puerto Rico.

There was a lot of media speculation around the event,

regardless. It was anticipated that either Wayne Lynch or I would win: I was the defending world champ and Wayne was touted as the hottest young surfer in the world. When the results were announced, however, a lot of people were left shaking their heads. Neither Wayne nor I won the contest.

In those days, the judges were using the same tried and proven rules that had been used since surfing contests began. The surfer who rode the biggest wave in the most critical part of the wave for the longest distance would be deemed the winner. That was exactly what Fred Hemmings did, in a copybook performance, taking my place as the new world champ.

Some say the judging criteria had yet to catch up with what was going down in the water. This may or may not be true, depending on which camp you're in. As far as I'm concerned, by the contest rules Hemmings was the winner, narrowly beating Midget Farrelly. Midget was smooth but old-school, safe, with not one critical turn in the whole forty minutes. Russell Hughes surfed really well into third place, showing his smooth, traditional style on some of the bigger waves.

Back before pro surfing came along, the World Championship was the most significant international contest on the calendar. In fact, it was the only one. It was held once every two years. In those days, the surfing world had a number of keen amateur officials and the International Surfing Federation (ISF) was in its infancy, lacking business-minded professionals, infrastructure and money.

The Puerto Rico event was within a hair's breadth of being cancelled when the president of the ISF, a Peruvian named Eduardo Arena, decided to flex a little muscle in New York. His business was importing the majority of the alcohol coming into Peru. When no sponsors stepped forward, Eduardo used his influence to get

Heublein, the distributor of Smirnoff worldwide, to put up the money for the event.

The Puerto Rican government and Heublein used their influence to get *ABC's Wide World of Sports* to cover the contest live and make a one-hour television special. This was the second time a television network had taken a serious look at surfing. The resultant program was a classic and is readily available on the internet. Shot on 35-millimetre film, the footage is still crystal clear with incredibly rich colours, just as it was when it first when to air.

On the production side, no expense was spared. The master himself, Greg MacGillivray, provided water photography, and following shots of fast-breaking waves were captured from a low-flying helicopter. A nosy New York scriptwriter was along on the shoot to make sure they got the story right, and the host was a household name in America, Mr Wide World of Sports himself, Bill Flemming. The writer easily identified the visual difference between the shortboard and the longboard as the happening issue in surfing. There was a priceless sequence of Flemming standing on the beach in a suit and tie, trying in ten words or less to explain the shortboard revolution.

Before the contest began, Wayne, Ted and I were travelling the world with Paul Witzig making his iconic surf movie *Evolution*. We had been on the road for more than two months, in France, Morocco and Portugal. I don't recall how many boards we made in France. We had free rein at Michel Barland's factory in Bayonne and the assistance of Jon, a lovely Basque man who ran the surf part of the factory. He understood how to glass and finish our boards, keeping them strong and light.

To say we were obsessed with trying to build the right board for the waves to fit our individual styles would be an accurate observation. Our biggest challenge in France was how to ride the break La Barre at the mouth of the River Adour. At 8 feet (2.4 metres) the wave was formidable, breaking on deepwater sandbars off a rugged breakwater just metres from ocean-going ships. In the beginning, I was riding a board I had shaped at Weber's factory in California. It had the latest American Lexan fin in a state-of-the-art fin box. The problem was that the fin was rubbery and would bend, causing the board to spin out whenever I cranked it off the bottom.

Wayne and Ted were also having problems with their Aussie-made boards. We would all head to Barland's shaping room as soon as we were out of the surf at La Barre. On any given day, we would go to the Biarritz markets for food, then surf, eat and shape, finally heading off to the Steak House to hear the latest records by the Doors and the Stones. The idea was that our new boards would let us turn harder in the pocket, pull in and harness La Barre's power. Over a few weeks, we all turned out boards that we were somewhat happy with.

It was on that first trip that I fell in love with the Basque area of France and its people. I have returned many times, and every one of those visits has been a fantastic adventure. On a few occasions, I have timed my trips to France to coincide with the Fêtes de Bayonne. Beginning in 1932, this festival has always started on the Wednesday before the first Sunday in August. On the Wednesday night, Bayonne's mayor literally throws the keys to the city from the highest spire, and from that moment, the city is officially open to all for five days.

It's actually five festivals in one and it's virtually impossible to leave, no matter how fatigued you are. From the running of the bulls to loads of Basque traditional dance, the whole city is alive with food, wine, energy and good cheer. Everyone wears white shirts and pants with a red sash, the same colours as for the running of the bulls in Pamplona.

One of my best friends in the Basque Country is a local dentist named François-Xavier Maurin, better known throughout the surfing world as FX. While staying with FX's family, I've had some amazing adventures at the Fêtes de Bayonne, losing hours and sometimes days under the effects of quality champagne and wonderful ambience. FX's wife, Dom, always lays out our red-and-whites, and she showed me how to tie the sash. A lot of private parties are held in houses acquired by societies that represent the city's guilds – the butchers, bakers, masons, etc. Each of these societies has a building with a fine cellar of champagne that has been acquired over many years. The only time the bottles are drunk with gay abandon is during the Fêtes de Bayonne. Everyone is full to the brim with music, good food and the finest wine. It is indeed the most wonderful festival I have ever been to.

When I think of FX and years gone by, I have to cast my mind back to the early days in Tahiti. Originally, the reason I ended up going there so often was because the Qantas flights from Sydney to Los Angeles could not make it in one jump. They had to stop in Tahiti for fuel, so getting off the flight was no big deal. You could spend as long as you wanted wandering all over Tahiti and the neighbouring islands before travelling on to LA. In those days, the airport in Papeete was a big grass shack – an impressive building more than 6-metres tall, but still just a grass shack. Every flight was met with Tahitian music played by a local three-piece group, with beautiful girls handing out frangipani/plumeria flowers and kissing you on both cheeks in traditional French style.

François-Xavier Maurin (right) and close mate François 'Murphy' Lartigau. *Alain Gardinier*

From left to right, me, Rene Begue and Sylvain Cazenave at Fêtes de Bayonne. *Photographer unknown*

FX and his family had a place in Raiatea, one of the most distant islands in the chain. The Qantas flights from Australia arrived late at night and my usual plan was to walk out of the terminal, find a patch of grass with some hibiscus to give me cover, and stretch out on my board bag. Then the next morning, I was first in line for the short flight to Raiatea. I must have done this ten times over a five-year period.

The runway was not sealed when I first visited FX on the island, and everyone in the town came out to greet the flight. It was a real social event. As the local dentist, FX was very popular. How he ended up in Tahiti is an interesting story in itself. After completing his dentistry degree in France, he travelled as a surfer to many far-flung destinations. When he was required to do his French national service, he was sent to the Marquesas Islands to practise dentistry. The waves were scarce there, as steep cliffs and deep water mostly surround the archipelago. Later, when a chance came up for him and Dom and their two young children to relocate to Raiatea, they jumped at it.

On my first visit, after an emotional reunion with my friend at the airport, we took off for his house, situated a couple of kilometres out of town and looking over the magnificent bay of Miri-Miri. FX and I surfed every day in high-quality left-hand reef breaks. We were the only surfers on the island. The entertainer Diana Ross owned one of the *motu*s, or small islands, that surround Raiatea, spread out in the lagoon every 800-metres or so. They are on the edges of passes that were created by fresh water running from the interior and down the sides of steep mountains. The volume of water in the lagoon eventually forced a break in the coral, and over time the channels became wider and wider. Some passes are a few hundred metres wide and perfect for surfing. The newer ones are narrow and difficult to surf.

Unbeknown to Diana Ross, her pass, Tehurii, was a perfect left, one of the finest I have ever surfed. It was consistent from 3 to 10 feet (1 to 3 metres) and was our go-to destination when we jumped into FX's little canoe with the outboard strapped to the outrigger. The other spot was Vial, which broke when the swell was bigger. A formidable big right, it broke in deeper water and looked like it could tear you apart if a wave managed to catch you off guard.

The safest and most convenient place for me to surf on my own was right in front of FX and Dom's house at Miri-Miri. It was a quality right-hander that rolled around the reef, quite docile compared to the other spots we regularly surfed. While FX was out doing his morning dentistry at the local school, I would often have breakfast and paddle the couple of hundred metres across the lagoon to the break.

On one particular day it was perfect: 4 to 5-feet (1.2 to 1.5-metres) and peeling down the reef, with only me out. At some point I must have touched the coral, because I noticed I was losing a little blood as I flicked off a wave and went back out. I paddled over a wave and noticed a shark fin just behind the blood, which was coming from my left foot. In the trough of the next wave I saw two, then three, then four sharks. They were all only 4 or 5 feet (1.2 to 1.5 metres) long but they kept getting closer to the blood.

In a pack, these blacktip reef sharks became more daring as their numbers grew. As I paddled through the crest of the next wave, I swung my board really fast and took off, running myself straight up on the reef, ripping off the fins and listening to the fibreglass being ripped open on the coral. I stood there for a long time, half an hour or so, trying to calculate if I could make it across the lagoon before the sharks realised where I had gone.

The blood on my foot looked like it had coagulated, so I hit the water like a machine, sprinting across that 200-metres back to the shore in record time. It took me a while to recover and tell my tale to FX, who immediately looked at the coral cuts, grabbed a couple of lemons and squeezed and rubbed them into the wound – apparently this kills the chance of coral infection. FX laughed as I screamed in pain. Regardless, I was stoked to have avoided my first serious encounter with the men in the grey flannel suits.

FX and his family eventually moved back to France, which was always hard for me to understand since he was such a committed Polynesian surfer. Back in France, his life was not the same. He had a partnership in a dentist practice in Bayonne, and by pushing himself could still get plenty of time in the ocean. But like every good Frenchman who works close to home, he would ride his motorbike back to the house for lunch with Dom. The roads in the area are very old and narrow and he came off his bike at a pretty good clip one day and then spent several months in the hospital with severe brain damage. FX is still not back to surfing, but he is improving every day. He still paddles a pirogue, though, which is a lifesaver. Hopefully one day he will once more be his old self.

Back in 1968, Wayne, Ted, Paul and I left France and arrived in Puerto Rico weeks before the World Championship. Our plan was to get acclimatised to the local conditions prior to the event. We had all the toys: boards that worked well to a greater or lesser degree, warm water and quality little waves to surf. They weren't big – 4 feet (1.2 metres) or so most of the time – and we surfed

Domes almost exclusively. As it turned out, 90 per cent of the contest was held at Domes.

Someone once told me that Puerto Rico was a protectorate of America, like a younger brother being watched over by the older. Turns out it is officially a 'commonwealth nation'. It seems to me that Americans have taken liberties with the definition of 'commonwealth'. Puerto Ricans can't vote for the president but are obliged to go to war to fight for America should they be called upon. With rampant unemployment, it is extremely beneficial that Puerto Ricans qualify for benefits, sort of like New Zealanders in Australia. Another similarity with New Zealand is that both countries are stunningly beautiful with lots of rain, and steep mountains in the interior.

Owning land there is easy for Americans, but verifying the boundaries of a particular parcel is difficult. Consequently, land tax for basic services is haphazard, to say the least. One friend of mine still can't verify his boundaries and has been waiting for the municipality to deliver a garbage bin for ten years. Obviously, basic services are limited because of the lack of funds for local government. My friend likes to refer to PR as a Second World country, as opposed to a Third World one; on many other Caribbean islands could be considered 'Third World' or developing countries.

Houses, hotels, apartments and shopping centres compete for every available inch of flat land all around the island's perimeter. The most interesting architecture is found in the clusters of houses clinging precariously to the top of every buildable ridge. No houses that I saw had any particular architectural merit, but they were strong, practical, and built almost exclusively of concrete and cut limestone to withstand the tropical hurricanes that wreak havoc there periodically. Their best quality is that their eagle's-eye positioning creates stunning vistas off every side towards the ocean. Narrow public roads are everywhere, linking the houses and getting you down to the beach. In many places, the ridgelines are only a few metres wide, plunging hundreds of metres into the jungle off both sides. When I went back to PR in 2015 for a week I didn't see a traffic accident, which is amazing because passing anything bigger than a small car requires one driver to stop and let the other crawl past. Everyone is extremely patient on the roads.

Unfortunately, agriculture is virtually non-existent in PR these days. Everything is imported except for the substantial bounty from the ocean. I would not say PR cuisine is fantastic by world standards, but they still manage to create their own twist on the unique Caribbean flavour.

Rincón is on the far western point of Puerto Rico and is the major surf hub. The big-wave break Tres Palmas is the jewel in the crown there. I have not seen this fabled wave in action but I have heard the stories. Maria's, which is also in Rincón, was the location for the final of the World Championship in 1968. It's not a particularly exciting wave, but it's great for a few rides on a long-board as the sun goes down. At the end of a ride, you have to pay attention to bits of shipwreck on the inside reef.

Further up the reef is Indicators. I surfed this wave on a red-hot locally designed shortboard built by a fellow named Jose. Both the wave and the board were exceptional. Indicators is a fast-breaking, challenging curl from take-off to finish. Around the point, just past the lighthouse, is Domes, the site of a decommissioned nuclear power plant. It's a series of reefs that twist and contort the swell into a wave that seems always to have something ahead of you.

Unfortunately much of the island was devastated by violent hurricanes in 2017, cutting power and infrastructure in the outlying areas for six months or more. Rincón was badly affected. One thing is certain: even with all the adversity, the PR surfing population is strong. All the local businesses are delighted to be a part of surfing festivities and the vibe in the bars and on the beach is relaxed.

Surfing has exploded in PR since my visit in 1968. Everyone in Rincón is surf-conscious. Hawaiian champion Fred Hemmings and I were invited to visit for a legends competition in January 2015, and the level of talent among the local shortboarders was world-class. We were the token 'personalities' at the event, brought in to shake hands, sign autographs and give some input on what could be done to improve the forthcoming fifty-year anniversary of the World Championship, scheduled for November 2018. Fred, who is a former Hawaiian state senator, gave a glowing speech at the civic reception. He praised the town and surfing, and everyone seemed to love it. Later that afternoon, I was having a beer with him and he told me an incredible story that I feel compelled to retell here.

As it goes, sometime between me winning the 1966–67 World Championship in California and Fred winning the next World Championship in Puerto Rico in 1968, the ISF president, Eduardo Arena, commissioned a silversmith in Peru to design and create a perpetual trophy. Eduardo personally paid in the vicinity of $20 000 for this piece of art, which bore the names of every former world champion. I cannot remember ever seeing the sculpture, but I have seen photos of Fred with a trophy featuring a proud silver surfer standing on a wave that towers over him. When Fred returned to Hawaii, he felt the trophy was too magnificent to be sitting in his home and deserved to be prominently displayed for all the people of Hawaii. As such, he presented it to the governor of Hawaii to display in his office. Naturally, he returned the trophy to the ISF for the next World Championship, in San Diego in 1972.

Jimmy Blears won that championship. Word is, he brought the trophy back to Hawaii and somehow it ended up in the hands of George Downing. Before he died, Jimmy confirmed that George had the trophy. Exactly why it was in his possession is unclear, but apparently Jimmy was not very responsible for a time, and for one reason or another George had the trophy to keep it safe and secure.

Due to the advent of pro surfing and the demise of the amateur world championship, the ISF fell by the wayside. Eventually Fernando Aguirre took over running the amateur championship, bringing it back to life. On numerous occasions, Eduardo asked George to return the trophy but George refused to do so. At one point, Eduardo even looked into hiring an attorney in Hawaii to recover it. Though many people have confirmed seeing the trophy in George's house, George, upon hearing about the possibility of legal action, began telling people he did not have it. He offered no explanation as to where it was.

A number of prominent surfers in subsequent years asked George to return the trophy, but he refused to do so. As would be expected, this upset Eduardo. Certainly the trophy is one of surfing's greatest artefacts and should be returned to the amateur organisation run by Fernando.

Several years ago, in an effort to settle the issue, Fernando had a smaller version of the trophy made. This did not satisfy those who knew the truth, and now that George is gone, it's hoped that someone can convince his son, Keoni, to return the trophy to the

International Surfing Association. It should be put into circulation again, presented to the world champion and then displayed at one of surfing's many museums around the world.

Fred Hemmings and Governor Burns of Hawaii, with the contentious trophy.
Photographer unknown

12

SUMBA

In May 2016 I was surfing in Sumba, Indonesia. I was staying at my friend Claude's new house, right next door to the five-star resort of Nihiwatu, where my daughter Nava and son-in-law Taylor had been married the year before.

The family joke is that I blew it by turning Nava on to one of the finest lefts in the world. She's a goofy-foot and will go anywhere to surf a high-quality left. Years ago, some friends and I were planning to go to Nihiwatu. I had already paid for two spots, thinking one of my sons would come with me. As it turned out, neither of my boys could make it so I offered the trip to Nava. She took a look online, saw the long-running lefts, and jumped at the opportunity. She's been addicted to the place since, so that's where she wanted her wedding ceremony.

Back in 1973, Claude Graves was a keen New Jersey surfer who
took a job with a big multinational construction company out of
Houston, Texas. The work took him to Indonesia. By 1998, he'd
had a gutful of the corporate world and he quit. Together with his
wife, Petra, he set out on an around-the-world mission to find the
perfect place to build a high-end resort. After travelling through
the Pacific Islands, they ended up back in Indonesia, eventually
hiking 130 kilometres along the desolate south-west coast of the
island of Sumba.

They finally found what they were looking for at Nihiwatu
(renamed Nihi Sumba in 2018). They could see the isolation would
be a problem for guests, but they kind of liked that. The wave was
amazing – a high-quality left, barrelling over shallow reef. Claude
didn't name his backyard spot anything. He just went surfing in
between working on the buildings. Eventually, the wave came
to be known as 'Occy's Left', made famous by footage of Mark
Occhilupo riding endless barrels there.

Claude and Petra decided that their high-end resort would have
a focus on all kinds of water sports as well as cultural and land-
based activities. They would do everything first class, and limit
the number of surfers to ten. They both thought it was important
to do the right thing by the impoverished local population, and
the Sumba Foundation was always a part of their business plan.
They started small, helping out the locals as much as they were
able. However, the challenge was so big that they needed more
help financially. Some of the guests made healthy donations and
the foundation was able to assist with equipping schools, providing clean water, planting teak forests and buying baby turtles from
the locals to set free (as opposed to the locals eating them). All
that, and they also provided employment to many of the villagers.

Over the years, the foundation has gone from strength to strength. As for the resort, after years of struggling, Nihiwatu began to make a profit. It seems some wealthy folks back in New York happened to have two sons who surfed. After they brought the boys to Nihiwatu and word spread, it became fashionable with the New York surf set.

Claude is a keen skier, like me, and he has stayed at our place in Sun Valley, Idaho. During one visit, he invited me to stay with him at Nihiwatu. Around April 2016, after the end of the ski season, I was in Oz surfing and hanging out with the family. Claude emailed a couple of times, then sent a message saying a big swell was about to hit. It had been big for weeks but, more importantly,

Perfect layout at Nihiwatu: the hotel Claude and Petra
Graves created, with amazing surf without crowds.
Jason Childs

almost no one who was staying at the resort wanted to surf the wave when it got over 6 feet (1.8 metres). He had to go to Bali, he said, and suggested I meet him there the next morning. In a panic Nava put it all together, organising tickets and transport. Claude met me at the airport and we flew to Sumba. When we arrived, it was exactly as he had said – there were a few surfers out, but really only a surgeon from Brisbane named Ian Martin was getting any of the quality bigger waves. A couple of talented older Brazilians were there too, but they soon left.

Nava on the nose while Taylor, Bryce and I check her out. This was the day of Nava and Taylor's wedding in Nihiwatu. *Rick and Paula Bickford*

For two days, Ian and I surfed 6- to 8-foot (1.8- to 2.4-metre) left-hand barrels alone. I was impressed with his surfing skills. He would take off on anything. At the end of the second day, Claude invited Ian and his lovely lady, Megan, over for dinner at his new pad on the point. Fantastic ambience – everything you could want after a day of 8-foot surf.

That night, I went to bed and woke up at 2 a.m. with stomach cramps. I stumbled to the bathroom, thinking I would pass whatever it was with a good bowel motion. Unfortunately I fainted on the dunny, nose-diving into the tiles and hitting my head on the windowsill on my way down. When I came to, I checked my forehead in the bathroom mirror and was blown away by the size and depth of the cut. It was serious – more than 5-centimetres long and quite deep. Nikiwatu is a huge resort, more than 460 acres (186 hectares), and I had no idea which bungalow belonged to Dr Ian and Megsy; I also decided I could not wake Claude or the maids in the house. Instead, I wrapped a towel around my head and went back to bed.

Before dawn the next morning, I took another peek at the cut and decided to go over to the hotel and find the resident doctor. I eventually found him and he took one look and told me in broken English that he had never done any deep stitches in the head. Thankfully he called his boss in Jakarta, who guided his apprentice through the ten stitches necessary to close the wound. It took him three hours to perform the job. I was grateful but when I got back to Claude's house and took a look, I could see it was amateur hour: there were big puckers of gathered skin between the stitches.

My wife was horrified when I stepped off the plane in Brisbane. Lucky for me, I was already booked in with a surgeon on the Gold Coast to correct a breathing problem in one nostril. When we walked into his office a few days later for the final consultation before nose surgery, he took one look at my forehead and asked what had happened. He thought I had been hit with a cricket bat. He offered to open and restitch the cut while I was under the general anaesthetic. Ti and I were quite happy with the end result, even though there is still a big scar in the middle of my forehead.

13

PERU

In March 2016, Eduardo Arena's secretary emailed me in Sun Valley asking me to take a call from Eduardo in Peru that afternoon, at 4 p.m. precisely. When I answered the phone, Eduardo's voice sounded more laboured than I remembered. He said he wanted to see me one more time before he died. I was taken aback. I'd lost a lot of friends, but no one had ever said that to me before. My answer was straightforward: I said I would do my best to come to Peru as soon as possible.

Eduardo was born on 20 March 1928, which made him eighty-eight when I got that call – a pretty good innings, as they say in cricket. He explained he was getting to the end of the ride. Fewer than 1 per cent of men in the Western world reach the age of ninety, he said. He was definitely not down about getting old – not one bit. In fact, quite the contrary. He simply wanted to see all his special friends who had mattered to him during his long life. Since I was one of his favourite sons, he was requesting that I come to see him. Naturally I would be his guest. He would look after everything. All I had to do was get to Lima.

Hanging out with friends at the Club Waikiki. From left to right, Alfredo 'Co Co' Granda, Ethel Kukea, Betty Heldreich Winstedt (behind Ethel) next to Roy Ichinos. Eduardo Arena with a uke. Unfortunately we don't know the names of the others. *Betty Heldreich Winstedt collection*

Senior Eduardo Arena on his throne. From left to right, Alejandro Rey de Castro (the son of Eduardo's sister), Pancho Aramburu, Alfredo Hohagen. *Ti Deaton Young*

In April, I changed my ticket home to Australia from Sun Valley and booked a route back via Lima and Santiago. As my departure drew closer, I started to watch the news about Peru with more interest than usual. Several weeks of torrential rain had created unprecedented floods that were devastating the entire country. There were images of people and animals being washed down

the streets of Lima. El Niño had wreaked havoc, which has happened every twelve to fifteen years going back as long as records
have been kept. There is archaeological evidence that the Inca and
Mochica civilisations were subject to the effects of El Niño. The
torrential rain and chain lightning strikes come predominantly at
night, and the coastal plains of Peru, which are normally barren
dust, quickly turn to deep, impassable mud.

I decided it was not a good time to visit. Eduardo was not
happy with me and said the media had exaggerated the situation,
maintaining that I should come, regardless. However, I stood my
ground, promising him I would come to Peru on my way back to
the States later in the year. This pacified him somewhat.

He explained that walking without assistance was becoming
increasingly difficult. Still, after his heart surgery the previous year,
he was in perfect health. On the surgeon's table, he had officially
been dead for two-and-a-half minutes. The doctors told him that
if you go for more than three minutes, you're out for good. You
can't keep the old bull down for long, though. Eduardo's father
had lived until he was more than 100, dying on the sole day in his
life that he was confined to his bed.

At the end of September 2017, Eduardo was still living in his
spacious apartment in Miraflores with his dynamic, wonderful
Peruvian girlfriend, Marita. He had two full-time nurses at home
and was using a motorised wheelchair. Both he and Marita were
riding in chauffeur-driven cars to get around town. He conceded
he was drinking too much but his doctor had confirmed that his
liver was in perfect working order.

So there I was on 9 November 2017, on my third trip to Peru,
sitting on the terrace of the luxurious Club Waikiki right on the
coast in Miraflores. I had just finished a good, hour-long surf on

a longboard at the break in front of the club. The last time I'd surfed there was 1965, when I was seventeen. Back then, there were thousands of seabirds diving for an abundance of fish. The Humboldt Current ensured the ocean was teeming with life. But in 2017, it was dead. Pollution and the smell of chemicals had changed Miraflores forever.

The population of Lima jumped from 1 million in 1965 to more than 10 million in 2017. Some things were still the same: the incessant rumble of thousands of small stones being rolled around in the shore break when I entered the water was exactly what I recalled from 1965. Back then, Eduardo was president of this prestigious club. He remained in that position for more years than anyone can remember. With 1200 members comprising almost all the upper-class families in Peru, the club is an oasis among the masses. Members don't pay any dues after forty years. All the amenities are state-of-the-art and upgraded consistently. On the surface, it looks exactly the same as the Outrigger Canoe Club in Waikiki, with two deep freshwater pools and a row of thatched cabanas. One of the beach boys, a 75-year-old named Mamico, was still there, waxing and taking care of the members' boards.

Other than the sea life, the only dramatic change I could see in the surrounding area was an eight-lane highway that had been built along the beachfront. The construction took place in 1978, under pressure from Juan Velasco's Soviet-Marxist government. They wanted to take back all the land from the club. That did not happen, but the amount of shoreline the club could utilise for access to the surf was reduced considerably.

The road noise was deafening, but the members I lunched with that day just smiled and said it was the price they had to pay for being allowed to keep their club. It looked to me like the prospect of running the gauntlet across the road to get into the surf would be hazardous, to say the least. However, that problem had been overcome by the employment of a full-time attendant and a designated crosswalk. The attendant walks out in front of the traffic with a sign instructing drivers to stop whenever a surfer wants to cross. I found it embarrassing – twenty vehicles screeching to a halt, horns honking, some drivers shouting abuse. Apparently there have been quite a few accidents. I did not feel safe. It was very different from 1965, when the beach boy would just wax your board and carry it down to the shore, over the pebbles, for you to hop on and paddle out.

I first met Señor Eduardo Arena in 1965 at the second World Surfing Championship in Peru. I'm sure he would not remember our first meeting, since I was the youngest member of the Australian team. That was my first time in a Latin American country. I was seventeen years old and impressed by the sophisticated culture. Eduardo struck me as the epitome of Spanish/Peruvian style – he had debonair good looks and was an imposing man, the alpha male at the Club Waikiki. With his distinguished mane of grey hair and his soft-spoken charm, he cut a very authoritative figure and had tremendous strength of character. Eduardo was elected in 1964 as the president of the International Surfing Federation during the first World Championship, in Manly, where the ISF had its first meeting. He served as such for its first ten years, and used his influence to make things happen all over the surfing world.

The next occasion I remember encountering Eduardo was in 1968, in Puerto Rico. We were becoming friends. Actually, it was more of a father–son relationship. I nicknamed him 'El Viejo'

Looking down from the deck of the Club Waikiki in Miraflores, before the Valasco government put in an eight-lane highway right along the beachfront. *Betty Heldreich Winstedt collection*

('Old Man') after he called me 'loco' ('crazy') on numerous occasions. The closing party at the Mayaguez Hilton was a huge event – 100 surfers and 200 associated friends. As I've already mentioned, Eduardo was a huge presence in the alcohol import business in Peru and, through a series of deals, he'd managed to get Bacardi to sponsor the party. A couple of hours into it, the manager informed him that there was no more free Bacardi being served – the budget had run out and everyone had to pay for their own liquor.

Sitting at the head table, Eduardo told the mayor and the government officials that it was strange of Bacardi to be so penny-pinching. They made rum, so why would they not supply plenty of their product? He then instructed the waiters to serve as much rum as everyone wanted – except that he told them to only serve Ronrico, the opposition product. It was Eduardo's way of letting Bacardi know how cheaply they were behaving. The next day, when he looked at the bill, he was cool but stunned by the amount: $15,000 for the Ronrico consumed at the party. He paid the tab gracefully, but I am sure the sales of Bacardi suffered in Peru.

During the Puerto Rican championships, I heard from the Australian team manager that Eduardo was becoming a little authoritarian in the ISF meetings. I did not attend them personally, but he reportedly pushed his opinions rather hard, getting involved in every aspect of the event. At the final meeting, all the representatives decided on a date and time for the event the following year in Australia. Once he was back in Peru, however, Eduardo discovered that the vintage for one of his wineries was coming in that same month and he promptly moved the date of the competition back by two months, notifying all the countries to make this adjustment to their calendars. Nothing was ever mentioned by any of the representatives – everyone accepted that Eduardo could do whatever he thought was best. He ruled with an iron hand.

At the 1969–70 World Championship in Victoria, we were all standing on the cliff overlooking the small, ragged swell at Bells Beach while the officials were trying to decide what to do with the competition. The main question of the day was whether they should wait or chase the surf down the coast. Normally, Eduardo would not get involved in these debates – they were way below him. On this occasion, however, he did get involved and the competition was moved hours away to the pristine beach of Johanna. As it turned out, it was a good call.

By the end of 1972, Eduardo had had enough and was ready
to pass the baton. Reluctantly, he held on for another two years
until the ISF could find the right person to fill his extremely big
shoes. It had been almost ten years since he'd taken the helm,
and the world had changed considerably in that time. The
Vietnam War was raging and young people were rebelling all
over the world. Just like a lot of young people, surfers were into
drugs. In Peru, cocaine was plentiful and cheap, and more easily
accessed than marijuana. When the Peruvian team travelled to
San Diego for the next event, in 1972, they brought their drugs
with them. Airport security was lax everywhere in the world in
the '70s. The parties associated with that contest in San Diego
were legendary, fuelled by big piles of white powder to kick the
festivities along.

Eduardo and many of the old guard were disillusioned by
these changes. All he could see was a sport that he had given his
life to being decimated. In his mind, something that had been pure
and clean was being compromised. He could no longer relate.
Consequently, he retired from the ISF, went back to his business
and life in Lima, and began dividing his time between his homes in
Lima and Miami.

Our relationship has blossomed over the fifty years since those
surf contests. I have visited Eduardo in Peru twice since that original trip in 1965 and he has always given me his energy and love.
I think of him as one of my father figures, providing guidance by the
style and length of his life. I don't have to speak to him all the time.
It's enough to know that he is there, living life to the fullest with his
impeccable grace and a definite attitude of not wasting a single day.

During my second trip to Peru, in July 2005, I visited him in his
Miraflores apartment, which overlooked the only eighteen-hole

golf course in Lima. Ironically, Eduardo never played golf, but he said the real estate was worth US$3000 per square metre.

This trip was interesting in that I was working for a French company called Bic Sport. It was owned by the two sons of its founder; they lived in Switzerland but had little to do with running it. Baron Marcel Bich gave the company to his boys after he developed the first production windsurf board. He was a man with a vision and did very well for himself by going to America straight after the war and inventing the first ballpoint pen. The reason it's not called a Bich and is called a Bic is because the marketing people on Madison Avenue advised him to drop the 'h'. The rest is history, as they say.

The operational head of the company in Vannes, France asked me to join the team and devise a way to lend some credibility to their moulded surfboards. It was going to be difficult. I had never believed in pop-out production boards. Irrespective of this, they invited me to France to look at the factory. The moulding system was amazing. The boards came out like plastic sausages and were virtually indestructible. Other than applying a cosmetic sticker and trimming the edges, there was little human-made energy in Bic boards. From a price point, however, they were the perfect entry-level surfboard.

Professional longboarding was struggling at the time. Competitors were hungry for any way to compete and make a few dollars. With this in mind, Bevan McKavanagh, Bic's surf division manager, and I came up with the 'One Design World Championship'. All the competitors would have to ride the same board, making it a very fair competition, and the judges would be of my choosing. Naturally I chose my heroes Mike Doyle and Joey Cabell, plus a French shaper, Gérard Dabbadie.

The first contest was held in the Mentawai Islands of Indonesia. We chartered five cruisers and invited thirty top surfers to compete in three separate contests at different breaks. Bic engaged a production company to do an hour-long documentary for French television. The promotion was a success, the program was entertaining, and sales of Bic longboards increased significantly.

When Bevan and I considered venues for the next event, Peru seemed like a good place to hold the contest. We needed someone to do all the organising in Peru so we hired Luis Miguel De La Rosa Toro, or 'Magoo' as he is known in surfing. He was a good choice. Magoo had surfed on the professional shortboard circuit in the mid-80s and could set all the infrastructure in place for the competition.

We held the event at Pacasmayo, an hour's flight north of Lima and the beginning of a chain of perfect lefts running from Chicama all the way to the Ecuadorian border. The surf was not particularly stunning, but everyone had a great time (especially when the hotel served the Peruvian speciality, baked guinea pig). One of the hottest competitors was Taylor Jensen from San Diego. I was really impressed with his style but unfortunately in the semi-final he fell on the rail of his board and split his ball bag – not badly, but enough to put him out of the competition unless we did something. It was a conundrum. Whichever way you look at it, Peru is a developing country. The town of Pacasmayo was primitive, and I was sure the local doctors would just crisscross him with stitches, even on his ball bag. On the other hand, I'd used superglue on both my sons many times, holding the two sides of an exposed cut together then running a bead of glue along the wound. So that's what I did for Taylor. We cleaned the cut with alcohol, dried it and repaired the wound with superglue, and he was back in the water in twenty minutes.

A couple of years later, my daughter Nava was competing in the annual longboard contest at Noosa Heads. She was at a party associated with the contest when Taylor came up and introduced himself, further saying that he knew me 'intimately'. This got Nava's attention. He went on to explain what I had done with the superglue in Peru and that was the start of an association that led to their marriage on Sumba in 2016.

Eduardo now uses a wheelchair for mobility. He's still very much alive at ninety years old, and when he has a point to make he is clear and strong even in English, his second language. It's easy to tell his mind is sharp as a tack.

14

SUN VALLEY

My whole family is addicted to riding fall lines – on skis, snow-boards, surfboards and skateboards. Anything to feel that pressure in a turn. For us, Sun Valley is the best place in the world to ride fall lines in the snow. How my wife and I discovered SV is an interesting story.

In 1982, I signed the contracts for the American TV rights to my movie *Fall-Line*, which was basically a documentary that detailed the similarities and differences between surfing, skiing, skateboarding and hang-gliding. The 48-minute film was crude in many respects but it was an accurate account of what I had dis-covered by participating in all these disciplines. The biggest thing *Fall-Line* had going for it was that it was the first movie to make the link between these activities. To my knowledge, I don't think anyone else had made a study of the commonalities and differences. Since then, the topic has been done to death by many more talented moviemakers than me, but I was the first and I am proud of the end result.

The contracts from Showtime paid a little under a quarter of a million dollars for unlimited rights on the 120-odd channels in their network. Ti and I had just been married, on 7 March 1982, at her family home in Palm Beach, Sydney. As part of our honeymoon we flew to Detroit and picked up a new motorhome for her mum, then drove it across America checking out ski resorts along the way. We intended to use some of the money from the Showtime deal to buy a house near a resort we liked in the Rockies.

I was also planning to buy an aeroplane. I'd been influenced by my close friend Max Schachenmann, who loaned me $60 000 to go out and buy an aircraft just before the Showtime cheque cleared. He was an experienced pilot, patiently showing me the idiosyncrasies of my new Maule Rocket and the avionics. After the ski trip I took lessons in LA and got my restricted pilot's licence. Max and I flew the little STOL aircraft all over Mexico, landing on beaches, surfing, camping out. He was right – the plane really stepped up my lifestyle. After some months of fun, we had the wings taken off and put the aircraft in a container, then sent it to Australia, where I flew for another 400 hours.

After looking at a few ski resorts in the Rockies, Ti and I ended up in Sun Valley, Idaho. My old surfing hero Mike Doyle had given me the name of the guy who made his single skis in Ketchum, next to Sun Valley. Michael Brunetto was firmly entrenched in the ski business. He had been in the industry since 1969, working for Head, K2 and the Ski. The mono or single ski was Mike Doyle's baby. With traditional ski bindings mounted side by side, it was difficult to ride. You had to stand parallel with your legs glued together.

Originally, Doyle had made them by hand for himself and a few mates, but the results were pretty unprofessional and very labour-intensive. Eventually he realised the boards needed machined, metal edges and a mounting plate. Unfortunately, it was almost impossible to achieve this without investing quite a few dollars into a plant and equipment. Doyle started to work with an entre-preneur named Bill Bahne in San Clemente, but that relationship only lasted a few months.

Mike Doyle with his invention. *Mike Brunetto*

As it turned out, Brunetto tooled up his factory to build the single skis for Mike. There wasn't much of a market, but people were talking about the design, especially in Europe, and more and more surfers were turning to the snow in winter. From riding waves, they understood the principle that you only needed one edge in a soft medium. Remember, there were no snowboards at this time, so for quite a few people the single ski was a good alternative in powder or slush.

Ti and I had started riding singles in the Australian winter of 1979 and were keen to get our hands on a precision-made board with a mounting plate, since one of the biggest problems we had was that we kept tearing the bindings off the deck. Brunetto and his co-workers welcomed us with open arms. Originally we were camped out in the parking lot at Warm Springs, but we were having some difficulty with the door on the motorhome – the volume of snow that fell every night made it tough to open the thing. Overall, the winter of 1982–83 was one of the best seasons for big snowfalls, with over 750-centimetres on Bald Mountain. Eventually, we moved the motorhome to Brunetto's factory – that way, we could plug in a power cord and also use the factory bathroom.

Ti and I skied our brains out every day on our new singles. We found untracked, lightly timbered glades where the powder had built up to knee-deep. Almost no one was skiing them. We used caution, staying in the trees on ridgelines most of the time and only riding the chutes when we were sure they would not slide. We rode like this for most of March and into April, being guided back to the lift by the sound of the live music playing at Warm Springs Lodge.

Brunetto tooling up to build single skis. *Mike Brunetto*

Bruce Paraguay aka 'Budda' on his single ski in Sun Valley. *Doyle collection*

Mike Brunetto – part Native American, and a talented pianist – was a very giving person. His mother had trained him classically, which let him improvise in any style. On a few nights, we were invited to his A-frame cabin in West Ketchum for dinner. He often cooked ducks he had hunted in summer, coupled with a sauce made from wild berries he had picked. Those were mouthwatering experiences that I will never forget. After dinner, he would play his beautiful grand piano.

Mike sponsored a hot young skier named Lane Parrish. We met Lane at Brunetto's Research Dynamics factory. He was good-looking and charismatic, worked as a stuntman in Hollywood, and was always trying new things to make his skis go faster. Mike and Lane were also hunting buddies. They were both excellent shots with a rifle or a bow and arrow.

On a fateful hunting trip in May of 1990, the two were flying home from Marys River Ranch near Deeth, Nevada. Lane was the sole passenger and Mike was up front piloting his Piper Super Cub. He had agreed to fly low over Salmon Falls Dam, where Lane's parents were camping. On the second pass, Lane turned around to take a picture of his parents waving from their campsite. He was wearing his favourite cowboy boots and got them stuck under the rudder pedals, which affected Mike's control of the aircraft. Even when he applied full power, he could not correct the yaw. Just like that, one wing struck the windshield of Lane's parents' pick-up and the next minute, Lane and Mike were upside down in 3-metres of water, 45-metres from the shoreline.

Exactly what happened next varies slightly from the two parties' accounts of the crash. It is a fact that Lane's parents, Christella and Leon, jumped in their little outboard tinny and motored out to the accident. Initially they had no idea who was involved, they were just going to help as quickly as they possibly could. It's hard to imagine the shock they must have experienced when they realised it was their only son. Mike says that Lane and he managed to free themselves and climb on top of the aircraft, laughing about what a close call they'd had. The Parishes say they could only see one person from the boat. As Christella and Leon approached the plane, they must have been frantic, overcome with grief. With all the drama unfolding, Christella fell out of the boat. It must have been an incredibly horrible situation, their worst nightmare. Brunetto says he jumped in and swam her over to the side of the aircraft. Unfortunately, both Lane and Michael were wearing lightweight flying suits and neither noticed that Lane's was caught in the door hinge of the plane. All of a sudden, the aircraft started to go under. The volume of water made it sink like a stone. Christella had a knife and she tried desperately to free the snagged material, Lane took the knife but it was too late, he only had time to look in his mum's eyes and say *Thank you*. In the final seconds Lane reached for Mike's hand but the weight was too great. Mike dove down trying frantically to free Lane's suit, but Lane drowned in Mike's arms, only 30-centimetres or so underwater. It was a tragic accident.

Mike told me that Christella said he was in such shock that he ended up floating face down in the water. Leon pulled Mike into the boat and saved him. Mike can't remember this happening – all he remembers after the accident is sitting in a tent on the shoreline, shaking violently from the cold.

It's a fact of life that tragic accidents can occur anywhere, anytime. When you live in the mountains, you have to be aware

Tommy Powel, Mike Brunetto and Lane Monroe hunting in the Wood River. *Mike Brunetto collection*

of the risks of ice, heavy snowfalls and avalanches. It's similar to living by the ocean, in a location where big, powerful surf breaks regularly. A certain percentage of us choose to spend extended time in these environments.

After my wife and I had looked at most of the serious ski resorts in the Rockies, we considered all the ingredients and it came down to either Jackson Hole or Sun Valley. For us, Jackson was too desolate and windswept and had no real village ambience. It wasn't the kind of place we felt comfortable. Plus it had a lot of short pitches with flats in between them and Ti and I both loved the constant pitch and long runs on Baldy.

Sun Valley had the village of Ketchum, which was an old western town first settled in 1880 by miners and Basque shepherds.

The Union Pacific Railroad came there in 1935, bringing well-heeled guests to stay in the Sun Valley Lodge and ski Bald Mountain. The first thing we really liked about the area was that it had two distinct ski areas: one for kids and beginners called Dollar Mountain, and Baldy, which falls vertically at varying degrees of steepness off every face.

Ketchum has a classic restaurant called the Pioneer Saloon. It has changed quite a bit since opening in 1954 but has kept its original flavour, with moose and elk heads hanging on the walls and a house speciality of thick steaks and giant Idaho potatoes. An old Santa Barbara surfer named Duffy Witmer made the Pioneer what it is today. It's a quintessential Ketchum watering hole, and everyone new in town has to go to the Pio during their stay.

We had two wonderful gay friends of Nava's staying with us one year, and naturally we took them to the Pio on their first night. When the food arrived, one of the boys, Pete, was astounded – the huge baked potato, full of sour cream and brimming with chives, filled his whole plate. He looked at it and said, 'Oh, my God, it looks like an elephant's vagina!' Needless to say, everyone at our table, and all the surrounding patrons, broke out in raucous laughter.

The Holding family has owned Sun Valley since 1977. They purchased the resort for a mere $12 million from a keen Californian skier named Bill Janss, who was running low on funds. Prior to this, the Union Pacific Railroad owned the resort. The company chairman, Averell Harriman, had been a driving force in the development of Sun Valley, but he lost interest in it after the board voted to discontinue the rail service in 1964.

Earl Holding was a self-made man who never lost sight of his humble beginnings. There are stories of him waiting tables and helping out in one of the kitchens. Earl and his wife, Carol, were fastidious – some would say fussy. Either way, the fact is that all of the renovations were done in first-class style, from marble-and-gold restrooms in the three grandiose log-cabin lodges to thick plush carpeting throughout.

The Holdings are a successful Mormon family with strong connections to the Church of Jesus Christ of Latter-day Saints. Both Earl and his wife were raised in the Mormon faith, and their three children follow the same religion. In 2013, Earl died peacefully at eighty-six years of age and his wife inherited all of his stock in the mountain and its parent company, Sinclair Oil. Today, Mrs Holding is still chairman of the board. Carol Holding turned ninety in February 2019 and by all accounts is still completely on her game.

When we first started skiing at Sun Valley, I vaguely knew another man who called Ketchum his home. Dave Robrahn was someone I had known of for a long time, but I don't think we ever actually met until Ti and I came to SV in 1982. He was an old Maroubra surfer and you sort of knew everyone that surfed in the very early '60s. After all, there were only a couple of hundred surfers in the Sydney metropolitan area.

Dave was a tall, good-looking goofy-foot. Just like many young people, he went in search of his dream and left Australia in 1968 looking for adventure. In the Swiss Alps he met a gorgeous blonde Bondi beach girl named Lorraine. They married in Biarritz, France in 1969. After the ski season, they spent the next six months working aboard sailboats, crossing the Atlantic to the Caribbean, then made their way up to Aspen, Colorado for the next winter. After that season, the pair ended up on the North

Shore in Hawaii, hanging out with another old Maroubra surfer named Ted Wilson.

Ted was blowing polyurethane foam blanks under an agreement with Barry Bennett, the surfboard tycoon from Brookvale in Sydney. Barry needed someone to go to Japan and set up the blank business over there for him. Ted suggested Dave and then put him through a crash course on how to build the infrastructure necessary to make foam blanks.

There was no surf industry in Japan in the '60s. Surfing was in its infancy, and most aspiring surfers only had access to boards that American military personnel had left behind. Barry Bennett was always thinking ahead of everyone else in the industry in Australia. He is one of the most successful men in surfing, and in Japan he was testing the market. Dave was his test pilot and he worked to make the concrete moulds, then began measuring out the chemicals according to the formula Bennett had given him. He experimented with the time it took to pour the liquid into the moulds before the foam started to expand. Getting the lid closed and bolted down in time was an arduous task that led to a few disasters, with foam billowing out of a half-closed lid.

After six months in Chigasaki, Dave had completed his task for Bennett. He trained a couple of locals to take over the business and he and Lorraine set out for Canada, where he joined the Whistler Ski Patrol before moving south to the Sun Valley Ski Patrol. The skiing on Baldy was really what attracted the pair to Ketchum. Dave became one of the best bump (mogul) skiers in the valley, which is probably the reason for his chronic back and knee problems.

When the snowboard was developed, Dave jumped right on it and never went back to skis. In his youth, he had completed an apprenticeship in Sydney moulding component parts, so officially he was a tool and die maker. With these credentials he found a job with Scott, the local goggles and pole company in Ketchum. Ed Scott owned 100 per cent of the company and Dave worked there for more than twenty years. Together with the head of R&D, an old Malibu surfer and mechanical engineer named Charley French, he helped design, build and test the first lightweight plastic ski boot.

Everyone agreed that the design of the Scott boot was fantastic, but the materials available in the '70s could not take the stress, so everyone broke a boot. The last time I put on my Scott boots was in Verbier in Switzerland. Ti and I were in the first cable car up Col des Gentianes, and 60-centimetres of powder had fallen. We took off from the top of the mountain, but three turns into the run my boot split across the top and literally disintegrated. Struggling down the mountain with only one foot attached to an 8-inch-wide (20-centimetre) single ski was incredibly difficult, and it took more than an hour to get to the village of Siviez and catch the bus back to Verbier.

Scott abandoned the ski boot business in the late '70s. Despite the problems with materials, however, Dave still considers Charley French to be a genius in mechanical engineering. After all, French was the main man with regard to the first non-fogging goggles, which were such a breakthrough for all skiers. He was also behind the strapless pole grip and many developments in mountain bike technology. Other companies rapidly copied his designs.

Charley is an amazing athlete and one of the fittest men I have ever known. Now in his early nineties, he still competes in triathlons and cross-country ski events, finishing ahead of athletes half his age and winning his age division in the World Championship.

Recently I was not surprised when I heard that he was competing in the Boulder Mountain Tour, one of the heaviest cross-country ski races in the world.

Dave Robrahn and Charley French. *Fiona Hickleman*

When Scott was sold to a Swiss company, they began to look into moving the head office away from Ketchum to Salt Lake City. Most of the Ketchum locals who worked there were not prepared to move to a big city, and in the interim, Scott put in a time clock for all employees. This was never going to work for Dave. He often worked in the middle of the night to get away from telephone calls. Unfortunately, the company could not accept this and Dave parted ways with Scott.

During his last few days in Ketchum, we drank a few beers and planned a road trip. We took off for Alaska, driving to Vancouver,

Barry Bennett, the Australian surfboard tycoon. This picture is from the '70s, however he is still working in his factory at eighty-seven years of age. Barry was awarded the Order of Australia medal in 2018. *John Witzig*

putting the car on a ferry and spending three nights travelling up the inland waterway to Haines. It was a great adventure with a good mate. We saw tonnes of wildlife – orcas, bald eagles, etc.

Unfortunately we didn't run across any bears, as it was winter and
they were in hibernation.

We also did some amazing heli-skiing. It was terrifying to get
out of the heli on a patch of mountain only as wide as the bird.
We had to inch our way around the front of the chopper, holding
onto the skids. Then the guide would tell us something technical
about the run, like not to ski straight down a chute but instead
make our turns wider on one side so that when the inevitable
slough tried to engulf us, with luck it would slide by and not
cover us completely.

Kent Kreitler is a legend in Ketchum, similar in status to Lane
Parrish. Both pushed the boundaries of what is possible when
skiing on Baldy. At forty-seven years of age, Kent is one of the main
pioneers of 'free-skiing', which has been adapted and adopted as
part of the Olympics and the X Games in the form of slopestyle
and half-pipe.

Free-skiing is also known as 'big mountain' or 'extreme'
skiing, and that was what Kent specialised in. A lot of people
have watched him tearing down unbelievably steep descents in
Alaska in various movies. He now enjoys part-time teaching and
mountain-guiding at the Sun Valley Ski School, in their 'legends'
category, which keeps him involved in skiing in a more service-
oriented realm and gives him time with his beautiful daughter.

I recall first seeing Kent in films made by Teton Gravity
Research and Warren Miller. Eventually I made his acquaintance
because we were both skiing the same out-of-bounds areas off
Baldy. One morning in the winter of 2017–18, I got on the lift with
Kent and he told me about a run he had skied the day before.

The chute falls into West Ketchum and is among the steepest in the valley. Kent traversed out a long ridgeline before dropping into 60-centimetres of powder at 45 degrees. The skiing was everything he expected until he came to a slight curve ten turns into the run. There, standing on the rocks just off to his right, was a full-grown mountain lion. It saw Kent and took off down the chute. About 20 metres further down the couloir there were four or five mule deer that the lion had been stalking. Naturally they took off down the chute ahead of the lion and Kent.

With powder flying everywhere on every turn, Kent kept trying to slow down to avoid running over the animals ahead of him. Eventually the lion ran off into the rocks and the deer scattered in the opposite direction. Kent made it to the river at the bottom of the run and put garbage bags over his boots to avoid getting wet, and a friend picked him up. As we were getting off the Warm Springs chair, I asked him if the run had a name. He replied that he did not think so – and so he decided to name it 'Hello Kitty'.

The resort of Sun Valley really likes having big groups come into town. It's good for everyone. They spend money in the restaurants and clothing shops and help keep the town afloat in leaner times. One group of unique enthusiasts who have come to town for many years is the National Brotherhood of Skiers. They only come for a week but boy, do they liven the place up. They blow in to have a good time, skiing and partying full-on.

Recently I was skiing the side country off Warm Springs in a few centimetres of powder. I was just sitting down on the chairlift to go back up the mountain when one of the Brotherhood came in hot and sat down beside me. We started to chat and he said he had seen me coming out of the trees at the end of my run and that he would love to ski some untracked snow. He said he was a ski instructor back east and felt confident he could handle any conditions Baldy threw at him.

After that line, I told him I was prepared to show him some out-of-bounds action since the snow was very stable and not too heavy that day. We ducked under the boundary rope at the top of the mountain and proceeded to ski across a relatively flat area to the top of a pretty steep chute called Heaven. On his first turn, my friend fell. He picked himself up but on the next attempt he fell again, and again, and again. I was concerned that I was getting him into something that could end up being a pretty serious situation, so I told him he should follow my tracks back under the rope and make the traverse to the machine-groomed run on Warm Springs' face. He was naturally disappointed, but was good-natured about our little misadventure. Later he invited me to one of the Brotherhood's parties. I had a ball, but have not seen him again.

One of the two things that brings the vibe down at any ski resort is rain. Rain is the curse. It's like onshore winds for surfing. The snow cover quickly breaks down, turning to slush and then into hard ice when it freezes overnight. This doesn't happen much in Sun Valley, but you can bet that at least once in any season you will wake up to it. Luckily we have abundant snow-making machines, which can put a cover over the ice.

The other element that brings the vibe down is uncontrolled development. The Holdings are investing more dollars in Sun Valley. A new high-speed quad chair is being installed up to Roundhouse from the gully below the Cold Springs chair, providing more access. It's debatable if this is a good idea: the area is steep, heavily timbered and rocky, which means it's prone to more slides and more accidents.

Until recently, Sinclair Oil was the cash cow that provided the finances to support Sun Valley. However, according to management, Sun Valley is now making money for itself and should continue to do so for the foreseeable future. Apparently Earl was a keen skier. I never got to see him ski, but I did experience his warm smile on many occasions when I got off the lift and went into the lodge on Seattle Ridge to warm up between runs. Earl regularly took a snowcat up from the Roundhouse and sat at the front door greeting everyone, happy that we were all enjoying his mountain. Now that he has passed, it is a bit up the air as to what his children will do with Sun Valley. Naturally we all hope it will be allowed to continue as it is, but none of the kids are keen skiers, so it may be sold to the highest bidder.

15

MOROCCO

The first time I was in Morocco was in the late autumn of 1968, shooting a sequence for *Evolution*. Ted Spencer, Wayne Lynch and I were travelling with the moviemaker Paul Witzig. We spent a month in France and slowly drove down the coast, camping out and surfing through Spain, Portugal and, eventually, Morocco.

Unfortunately we did not get very far down the Moroccan coast – only as far as Kenitra, which has a rocky breakwater offering some protection from the north wind. Apparently this was the first place surfed in Morocco, back in 1952. It was the only place we had heard about. After our trip, the surf potential in this part of the world was exposed by other travelling surfers and photographers through reels of movie footage and stills. When I saw those images, I was amazed by what the right-hand point breaks looked like just 160 kilometres south of where we had been.

I returned to Morocco in the winter of 2017–18, nearly fifty years later. I was travelling with Ti, my son Bryce and one of his best mates, Tully Byrne. This time we flew down half the length of the country to Agadir. First, though, we scheduled a layover for a night out in Amsterdam.

I hadn't visited that city since 1993, when I was the surf team manager for the French clothing company Oxbow. On that run, Joel Tudor, Duane DeSoto, Zack Howard and my son Beau were being rewarded for six weeks on the road doing promotions every day, crisscrossing Europe from Italy to England. Thinking back on it, I don't believe Joel, alias 'Boris', was with us by that stage – he had run off to London with the roadie's girlfriend, Angelique. But that's another story; I think I covered it in *Nat's Nat*.

After a successful tour promoting the brand, we felt that a weekend off in Amsterdam was a justified reward for the boys. A local named Anjo Daemen, who was the Oxbow importer in the Netherlands, owned a chain of coffee shops called Spare Time, and he organised our visit perfectly. Everything went as smooth as silk.

The first evening was memorable. We met him in his flagship store in the heart of the old city. When he asked what I would like to smoke, he told me I could name any region in the world, any year, and he was confident he would have that particular type of marijuana in his vault. After some debate with the boys, I nominated Durban Poison from 1969 as my personal favourite. Anjo promptly guided me downstairs into his underground cellar, past rows and rows of sealed glass drawers. I could see that everything within them was clearly labelled. Anjo was obviously a connoisseur.

As we moved down the aisles, I commented that I had never seen marijuana stored like wine. His cellar was extraordinary. When we came to the South African section, Anjo halted to confirm the year of my preference. His Durban Poison looked exactly as I remembered it. I squeezed one green, sticky head and smelt my fingers, and the odour was exactly the same as it had been in Africa all those years before.

Anjo took out a small quantity of the weed and we walked back upstairs to join the boys. The actual stone of the high-quality sativa was also just as I remembered. After an hour of smoking, we were all well and truly loaded and ready for a night on the town. It's hard to choose one incident that stands out. We visited every bar we could find before ending up in the red-light district in the early hours of the morning. I recall the women were beautiful and exotic, with skin colours from jet black to porcelain white.

My return trip was different, of course. I endeavoured to find Anjo and Spare Time coffee shops, but to no avail. Too much time had passed, I suppose. I'm sure Bryce and Tully would have loved a glimpse of Anjo's world, but it was not meant to be. They discovered their own Amsterdam, arriving back at the airport just before we boarded the plane for Agadir.

I feel compelled to make a note here on Amsterdam Airport, which is by far the best I have experienced. It is different from every other airport – the toilets are spotless, it is well designed, and everything works, despite it being one of the busiest airports in the world. The Dutch have considered the comfort of their visitors first and foremost. They don't even have boring, straight-line conveyor belts at security: instead, they have soft curves to take the edge off. They've also installed well-designed, contoured seats to sit in while waiting for your flight. The place is a pleasure.

I can't remember everything about my trip to Morocco in 1968. I do recall the kief, which is Moroccan hash. A more accurate name for it would be 'laughing powder'. Wayne, Ted, Paul and I would roll around in hysterics after eating dates laced with the stuff. I also remember the aroma of the pungent green mint tea that the locals seemed to drink all through the day. It was a pleasant beverage after a surf to rinse the salty taste from your mouth. I am pleased to say this tradition is still carried out.

On that first trip we donned local garb, wearing our djellabas for weeks on end. The garments were loose-fitting and comfortable, covering us from head to toe and providing excellent protection from sun, wind and sand. In 1968, everyone wore them. Not so much these days, but you still see quite a few people wearing traditional dress out on the streets.

It's not hard to understand why Europeans have invaded Morocco. It's a miraculous country. Everywhere you look, tourists are crammed into hotels and restaurants, which is a good thing for the economy. Tourism is the number one economic force in Morocco. In the Agadir area alone, there are more than forty surf schools.

The resort where we stayed in Taghazout had five hotels with a total of 140 beds and was run by Surf Maroc, which is owned by two inspired surfing Englishmen who saw a hole in the market in 2001. By offering good service at the right price, they have been very successful. Our guide was Ilyass Masrour, the son of a Berber mother and an Arabian father. Ilyass speaks perfect English and is an excellent surfer, with a broad knowledge of Moroccan culture and history.

Tully and Bryce being dinosaurs. *Ti Deaton Young*

Dinosaur footprint at Anka Point. *Ti Deaton Young*

Out in the water, the majority of the punters seemed to be Englishmen, ranging from complete beginners to weekend warriors. The surf season starts in winter and runs from October through to April. Jimi Hendrix spent time in this area in the 1960s, coming originally to perform at the Gnaoua World Music Festival, which is held in June each year. Jimi bought a house in Aourir and nicknamed the town 'Banana Village' because of the number of banana plantations.

The soft, rolling beach breaks at Banana Village are a perfect place to learn to surf. Just a few kilometres away, however, on the very same day, there can be 8-foot (2.4-metre) driving barrels. That's how it was the week we visited – the loads of cute Pommy girls returning from their beginner lessons juxtaposed against our family dragging themselves into the hotel after a day of surfing heavy waves at Anchor Point and Draculas.

Just getting in and out of the water was life-threatening. After we clambered down the 2.4-metres of vertical, jagged rock along the bluffs, the next phase entailed more rocks, edged like dull razor blades. We found you had to avoid putting too much pressure on the soles of your feet – essentially you had to walk flat-footed across them without making any sudden movements, all while navigating barrages of whitewater.

I stayed on the cliffs at Draculas, content to watch Ilyass and Bryce fly down the line with astonishing speed. I ended up in a conversation with eight Israeli surfers. It was heartening to see that in this day and age, with so much tension between Arabs and Jews, a troop of Jewish surfers could travel to a Muslim country and everyone could feel comfortable – locals and visitors alike. They took the time to explain to me that they were surfers first and foremost. They saw surfing as their religion; it was as meaningful to them as Judaism.

The Agadir market. *Ti Deaton Young*

Bryce skating around the French girls, Lee Ann Curren in white. *Richard Inskip*

The quality of the waves in Morocco, compared to other places in Europe, is outstanding, and there are many surfers there these days. Anchor Point is about forty-five minutes outside of Agadir and a world-class right-hand point break. There were probably fifty people in the water when I paddled out the first morning – surfers from every part of the world. I heard Spanish, Dutch, Danish, English and Russian being spoken in the take-off zone.

Driving back from our first session at Anchor Point, Bryce spied a skate park directly up the hill from our hotel. Since he never travels anywhere without a skateboard, he was in heaven. Ilyass explained that in 2017, a group of professional skaters came through town and decided they wanted to give something to the kids in Taghazout. Not only did they fund the skate park, they also put in the actual man-hours to build it. The design is world-class and the finish is perfect. One of the builders must live close by: twice a week he turns up at an appointed hour with twenty boards in his van and all the kids line up to have their turn. This works out really well, since they learn to both skate and share the equipment.

The next day we drove north of Taghazout to Safi. At every town we ran the gauntlet of being stopped by the police. They were not nasty, however. Some even smiled. Basically, they just wanted the car's registration and Ilyass's licence number. Crude villages dotted the coast road. A lot of the buildings looked to be in ruins, the result of a change in the law in 2010. Prior to this, Moroccan citizens could build ramshackle dwellings out of anything they could find. There were no building codes or licences, so they could erect a house anywhere they chose to squat. After the law changed, the government bulldozed many homes whose

Bryce flying down the line at Draculas. *Clair Gaya*

owners had not acquired the land legally, and left other houses
standing but abandoned.

Argan trees lined each side of the road. These trees are incredibly tough, with sharp spikes. Even the local goats are challenged
to reach up more than about 30-centimetres. About once a year,
the argan produces a beautiful yellow flower. Every part of the
plant – the buds, flowers and leaves – is utilised for its oil, which is
prized all over the world and is a major export of Morocco.

After four hours on the road we arrived in Safi, a big industrial
city that ships superphosphate internationally. The local processing

plant is a heavy polluter, belching thick white smoke constantly. The best break in town is nicknamed 'the Head of the Snake' and is quite possibly the best point break I have ever seen – a 275-metre-long barrel. When we surfed it there were fifty boogie-boarders in the line-up, all with an amazing ability to negotiate the tube.

Ilyass explained that the explosion in boogie-boarders came about because back in 2004, four local boogers were invited to surf in the International Bodyboarding Championships in Hawaii and this development was brought to the attention of a Moroccan philanthropist, who decided to support each of the surfers with a sponsorship of $140 000 for two years. Then he extended the deal for another two years. Anywhere in the world this would have been regarded as a very generous grant, but in a developing country it was extraordinary. Some of the boogers used the windfall to achieve great things for themselves and their families; others indulged in all the vices they could find until the money had been pissed up against the wall, then they returned to poverty. Either way, in the wake of

Ilyass's deep backside carve at Anchor Point. *Alex Posting*

their great fortune, boogie-boarding became incredibly popular in Morocco. Every local sponger lives in hope that he will come to the attention of a rich benefactor and ride the tube forever.

Ilyass Masrour and his wife Aida. *Mustapha Elbaz*

At the top of the 800-metre descent to the beach, you are asked to pay an entrance fee to drive down a rough track. When I asked Ilyass where the money goes, he wasn't sure. All I can say is that the dirhams do not go into infrastructure. There were no toilets anywhere – all the campers and daytrippers were forced to shit in the bushes. I found the smell of shit and the amount of litter staggering.

Unfortunately, the ugly side of Safi extended into the water. Localism seemed to be out of control. The day we were there we witnessed four fistfights – three in the water and one in the car park. As well as the boogers, there were about 100 stand-up surfers all jockeying for position. It was madness. Bryce caught a few big solid barrels but on every wave he caught, another surfer dropped in. Finally he got a wave through to where I was sitting. A surfer paddling back out turned and took off on Bryce and then, when he fell off, he threatened Bryce, ordering him to the beach. In an hour and a half I caught one wave that wasn't particularly memorable and had a couple of take-offs. There were talented surfers from all over Europe and North Africa in the line-up, mainly Moroccans, French, Spanish and English. A few too many Brazilians, with the odd Aussie or American, rounded out the mix, all of them paddling for every wave. It seemed like everyone had heard a swell was coming, the biggest of the season.

It was too much aggro for us. After one surf, we left and started driving south towards Agadir. Twenty minutes into the trip, we stopped to check a wave that looked like it could be possible to surf. It was a big right-hander, breaking 360-metres off the end of a rocky point. The people who lived there told us that it had never been surfed. It looked daunting, but Bryce told me he needed to get in the water – he *had* to surf after what had happened at Safi. He needed a reality check, he said.

As he made his way out to the shore, he disappeared behind the point and we could not see him searching for a place to enter the water. Then, after twenty minutes, we spotted him paddling over a set hundreds of metres offshore. After a couple of smaller take-offs, he jagged one amazing big barrel and rode it all the way to within 90-metres of us. As the wave exploded against the cliff face, Bryce somehow managed to get back up the cliff without being flayed on the rocks. All the villagers started clapping. It was like a scene from *The Endless Summer*.

Thinking back on it, that trip to Morocco created a major shift in my views about what I could and couldn't do for the rest of my surfing life. There are just too many people surfing anywhere that is easily accessible. If you want quality waves, you have to pay for exclusivity. Kelly Slater's wave pool is making more sense. In my seventy years, I don't think I have been scared to take off many times, but recently I've found that sometimes I don't go out because I know the conditions are out of my realm. It's not just the size – it's about the volume and power, and an understanding of what a wave is capable of, that the repercussions can be dire.

Something has changed in me. I guess now I know the consequences of one little miscalculation in a deep tube. I am more wary. I think I know my limits, even though I still have that desire to commit and pull into the tube. This inclination is ingrained in me, as it has been for sixty years. I just think that in the last two years, mentally and physically, I've lost some of the ability. It's been two years since I've had a tube I could ride inside for a long enough period of time to relax and appreciate the unique situation I was in. I hope it occurs every time I go in the water, but the green room has eluded me these last few years.

I am forced to come to terms with the fact that I cannot surf substantial waves any more. In Morocco, I found I was doing what I always used to laugh about: paddle one stroke forward, look over the front, and paddle two strokes back. It's what happens when you really don't want a wave of considerable volume.

I've had a lifetime of extraordinary experiences, but maybe I've finally had my fill.

November 2018. So far I am the oldest guy to ride Kelly Slater's Surf Ranch. *Young family*

16

THE END OF
AN ERA

I am writing this from a bed in the Wesley Hospital in Brisbane while recovering from the work of the talented Dr Benjamin Forster, who has wielded his knife through my left knee and given me a total knee replacement.

The cold hard facts are that it will take at least six weeks of rehab until I am back in the water. I won't be standing, mind you: at best, on my return to the ocean I'll be lying on a boogie board. What an embarrassment. I'll be a 'speed bump', as Donald Takayama used to call them, implying that boogers don't stop you when you run them over. The funny thing is that along with knee-boarders and bodysurfers, they're the real backbone of surfing. They're the ones who do it with total conviction, riding as deep in the curl as possible.

My estimate of six weeks before paddling out is based on Tom Carroll's experience. He had the same surgery with the same prosthesis, and is now back riding waves on a mat. Tom's report was another push – or a shove, really – for me to get this procedure. Apparently he was having knee problems, not serious, but he couldn't straighten his leg, which was an alarming development at the age of fifty-six.

Tom's a charger – no wave is too big – and wants to surf into his eighties or nineties. Years ago, he wiped out and ruptured his anterior cruciate ligament and medial collateral ligaments and I went and visited him in Mona Vale Hospital. Tom's had a lot of accidents; so have I. Most fully committed surfers have. At this point in history, we don't know how long a high-performance surfer can keep doing it – putting everything back together and paddling out to do it again. It's totally new ground, and seems to keep shifting to later and later in life with each generation of surfers. One thing that is interesting from Tom's and my observations is that the first knee to break down is your front, driving leg. Tom is a goofy-foot, so his right knee was the problem; I'm a natural foot, which means my left knee was the weak link.

For years, the X-rays and CAT scans showed no cartilage at all on the inside of my left knee, and very little on the outside. It was bone on bone, baby. The big-time surgeon in Sydney for knees is Dr David Wood at the Mater Hospital, a lovely man who trimmed my menisci many years ago.

Some five years ago, when the pain in my knee became acute, Dr Wood sat my wife and me down with two or three wannabe specialists from around the world who were studying under him. These aspiring surgeons were hanging on his every word as he explained my position. He said that with a particular implant he liked to use, I would be pain-free. I'd be skiing again within six months, and golfing would be easy. When it came to surfing, however, there were no guarantees. He didn't think it was going to be possible to jump up to my feet from a lying-down position as quickly as necessary.

We were devastated. Ti and I definitely weren't going for his brand of prosthetic knee. It has always been the spring to your feet that is critical to catching a wave – a difficult act to master, even when your knees are in perfect condition. As I've grown older, jumping up has become harder. I am not alone in this; it seems everyone has the same problem. When I get back from five months in the snow, for instance, I spend the first ten days in the water going over the falls on every other take-off until it all comes back together. A lot of it is timing, but it's essentially the physical act of jumping up.

With our heads hung low, my darling wife and I left Dr Wood's office and flew back up the coast. His parting words were that he would 'get me in the end'. I laughed but realised there was no way I was going to dodge the bullet. He told us about a product called Synvisc I could use as a stopgap. Its active ingredient is hyaluronan, which is found in the wobbly part of a chicken's comb. It sounds weird, I know, but I was desperate. Back in Angourie, we ordered it online and had the magic elixir delivered to our local doctor's office. When it arrived, the thick, golden liquid looked like honey. Our friend Dr David Hope injected me with a huge needle, slowly pushing the fluid into my knee joint. I felt the relief straight away and walked out of David's office totally elated. I had three Synvisc shots a year for the next two years, but the last time I went in for one, I got up and the pain was still there. David and I locked eyes and we both knew it was time for Plan B.

Plan B was stem-cell therapy – or poor man's stem-cell therapy, actually. In the industry they call it PRP, or platelet-rich plasma, therapy. Before that, though, in 2014 an old friend suggested I see Dr Tony Delaney at the Narrabeen Sports Medicine Centre. I was on my way to France to compete in a father-and-son surfing contest with my boy Beau. Dr Delaney's specialty is orthotics, and he made me a pair for the inside soles of my shoes on the spot. The idea was to correct my walking and my stance in general. Building up the inside of my shoes would help correct the rubbing of the joint between my tibia and femur.

Romain and Danni Maurin. Perched on Daddy's shoulders, the look on Danni's face says it all.
Hoalen collection

We built this 10' 4" tank on the farm to get me standing up again after the knee replacement.
Ti Deaton Young

The relief was almost instantaneous. In Paris I was walking
around and getting on and off the metro like a grommet. Since
that time I've had orthotics in all my shoes, from ski boots to work

boots, to my thongs for going down the beach. There is a theory Dr Delaney told me about that proposes that men get more bow-legged as they get older, while the opposite occurs for women, who get more pigeon-toed.

After the orthotics, the next step was PRP. Opposite Hornsby Hospital is Dr Toos Sachinwalla, who is totally committed to PRP therapy. What he did was take 60 millilitres of my blood, then separate the platelets, or heavy bits, by spinning it in a centrifuge. He then injected the remaining platelet-rich fluid back into my knee joint. The idea is to stimulate and promote healing by slowly building new cartilage. The PRP, which is rich in natural growth factors, is kind of like fertiliser.

I had four treatments of PRP a month apart and was more than happy with the results – another two years of relatively pain-free surfing and skiing. It's funny: I had minimal discomfort when actually doing these activities, but there was still acute pain on occasion. The big issue was walking, particularly downhill, and it's 100 steps to the Point from the car park near where we live. I had not walked down those steps in more than two years, instead taking the car and driving to the back beach.

Sleeping was also uncomfortable – I had to prop my left leg on a pillow. Basically, my knee was always hurting a bit. Getting up from a sitting position was like an electric shock. There was no way I could work on the farm: after six hours of getting on and off the tractor, fencing, and picking up rubbish, I would have to spend the entire next day on my back, recovering.

In 2016 I knew it was time for a total knee replacement. The first thing I had to do was gain all the knowledge I could about what prosthetic knees were available. I found out it's a bit like buying a new car: there are approximately ten manufacturers

offering everything from a street car to a four-wheel drive. It's not
that one is necessarily better than the other; it's a matter of finding
out which is the best one for the activities you want to do after the
operation.

Nava and Taylor and their first daughter, Jagger, usually spend
five months of the year at our Angourie home. When Taylor was
back in California in September 2016 for sponsor obligations, he
found himself sitting out the back at Malibu one afternoon on a
solid south swell, talking to a fine 59-year-old ex-pro named Allen
Sarlo. Allen told Taylor about his own recent knee replacement
and Taylor lit up, describing my knee issues and pressing him for
more information. Allen had only had his operation six weeks
earlier and yet was out surfing on a shortboard. 'Ripping' was
how Taylor described his surfing.

When Taylor arrived back in Oz he told me the details and
handed me Allen's phone number. I called Allen that same day and
he relayed the name of the company that made his prosthetic knee:
Smith & Nephew. The model name was the Genesis II.

Sarlo was over the moon with the results. He passed on the
name of the surgeon in Santa Monica who had performed his
operation. As an Australian citizen, it was cheaper for me to have
any operation in Oz, not to mention being able to recover at home
with my family close by, so I called Dr Wood instead. He told me
the Genesis II had not yet been approved in Australia.

Some twelve months later, on Instagram, I learnt that Tom
Carroll had had a total knee replacement. When I called him,
he told me his prosthetic knee was a Genesis II, the same as
Sarlo's. I called Tom's doctor and was surprised to learn that he
had somehow been using the Genesis II for more than two years.
I immediately made an appointment.

I've kept in contact with Sarlo, quizzing him about his path to full recovery. The last time we spoke, in May 2017, he was on the North Shore of Oahu and had been surfing Sunset during the last north swell of the year. He said he was surfing hard, jumping to his feet 'as quick as a shithouse rat'. Someone out in the water told him his cutback looked just like mine. I felt pretty chuffed, as Allen is a great surfer.

In an email to Dr Ian Martin and his wife, Megsy (my friends from the Sumba trip), I just happened to ask if they knew any top-line orthopaedic surgeons for knees. Ian said he did, and that was how I was introduced to Dr Ben Forster. Not only did he have a great reputation, but it also turned out he used the Smith & Nephew Genesis II.

So here I sit in Wesley Hospital, loaded full of morphine, wondering how long it will take for this new knee to feel a part of me. So far, the pain is not bad. The only problems are the constipation from the heavy drugs, and the catheter sticking out of my penis, draining my urine whenever my bladder feels inclined to empty itself. Amazingly, the physio at Wesley had me up and walking within three hours of the operation, but I am expecting that the road to full recovery will be long and painful. Therefore, it is the perfect time to work on this book and hopefully turn out something that will be entertaining and, with regard to this chapter, also help out a few surfers with their own knee issues.

As I've mentioned many times, I have always liked good surf stories, especially when they have a twist. In that vein, I want to share the response from my old hero, the now 75-year-old Mike Doyle, when I told him I was having knee surgery. 'Join the club,' he wrote. 'I had my neck fused three months ago. This Friday, carpal tunnel on wrist and elbow. July 7th, lower back surgery with pins, rods, screws and plates. I can hardly walk, all bent over. It's tune-up time, laddie.'

Out in the surf on my last day before surgery, Bryce asked me what they were going to do with the old knee when they took it out. I really hadn't thought about it, but after some discussion the family were adamant they didn't want it disposed of. It had served us all well for nearly seventy years, they reckoned, so they wanted it pickled and taken to the farm, just like the snake that bit Nava years ago. Dutifully, I communicated their request just before I went under. Dr Forster said that returning body parts was not legal but that he would take a few pictures of my knee as a remembrance.

My hero Mike Doyle (1941–2019) and his beautiful wife Annie. **Doyle family**

Postscript: It is now almost fourteen weeks since the operation. For the past month I have been surfing, but only lying down. I started on a soft board then graduated back to one of my high-performance Burch asym concaves. Last weekend I made the leap, literally: I jumped to my feet for the first time in three months and two days, with no pain, which felt fantastic. I built a board on the farm just to make it easier. It's 10 feet 4 inches (3.1 metres) long by 23 inches (58-centimetres) wide and is stable and very forgiving. As Tom Carroll advised, I've been practising on the carpet. I feel just like Gidget, taking a good breath and jumping up.

Send them up, Huey! I'm back.

North swell on the North Coast. *Photographer unknown*

ACKNOWLEDGEMENTS

With thanks to the following people for help with direction and original editing: Ti Deaton Young, Peter Ellem, Alex Wilson and John Witzig.

All photographers have been credited wherever possible.

Special thanks to: Nyarie Abbey, Richard Harvey, Ron Turton, George Greenough, Bryce Young, Ti Young, Nava Young, Taylor Jensen, Luki O'Keefe, Ryan Burch, Scot Innes, Denny Aaberg, Fiora De Castro, Aida and Ilyass Masrour, Robert 'Wingnut' Weaver, Rachel Platt, Valerie Evans, Tom Carroll, Andrew Stark, Garry Birdsall, Dick Evans, Alain Gardinier, Craig Leggett, Mike Hynson, John Grannis, Bob Smith, Dana Nicely, Terry Murphy, Shea Weber, Brian Hughes, Terry Wall, Robert Conneeley, Fred Hemmings, Miguel Plaza, Dom and FX Maurin, Claude Graves, Eduardo and Marita Arena, Ken Oliver, Bevan McKavanagh, Michael Brunetto, Mike and Annie Doyle, Kent Kreitler, Richard Inskip and Tim Baker.